Contents

FAITH CAFÉ EDITORS: Kristi Cain, Laura Derico | WRITER: Chris Maxwell | DVD VIDEO PRODUCERS: Charles Powell, Michelle Wheeler

Introduction

Not very long ago I heard two radio show hosts discussing an experiment they had recently performed where they randomly interviewed individuals in Christian ministries, asking them if they could name all of the Ten Commandments. Few could name more than seven. The question that left me asking is this: In a culture in which education and knowledge are worshiped, why has a thirst for biblical understanding not spread to the common Christian?

This awareness triggered our decision to focus these episodes of Faith Café on something as seemingly basic as the Ten Commandments. The first segment looks at the direction God has provided for us, how his words to "A Man and a Nation" reveal his character and his desire for us to follow him, first and only. The next segment focuses in on what distracts us from keeping God first: "Words," "Work," "Family," "Hatred," and "Fantasy." Finally, we'll look at the kinds of deception that we engage in: stealing from and lying to others, as well as ourselves.

My pastor preached a sermon in which he made the bold statement that pride is the reason we fail to follow the first commandment and that this commandment is our foundation, meaning essentially that if we can obey the first one, we can obey them all. The more I listened to him, the more I agreed. Perhaps pride is our problem. Pride, after all, distracts me from keeping God first. Instead, it encourages me to satisfy myself before anyone else—and that's where the problems begin.

So I encourage you this quarter to do more than mechanically go through the lessons and practice the disciplines. Examine your heart. Allow God to search you and get rid of your pride. When you encounter a command that you don't like or consciously violate, ask God, "Why am I struggling with this?" Let him use these commands to inspire you to take the hard shell off your heart as he works to shape you into a pliable but powerful servant whom he can use to change lives.

ENTER

In our gatherings we do not want you just to sit back and listen. Faith Café invites you to enter into an environment where it is safe to ask for and seek answers. Phrases lure your mind toward deeper paths; quotes dare you to stare into your real self; questions give you a chance to talk to yourself and your friends about what is relevant in your lives.

DRINK

This segment highlights portions of Scripture to help you gain a better understanding of truth, while friends beside you voice their own reflections about how the biblical story inspires them to believe in new ways. Your soul can be refreshed by drinking in the living water of God's Word.

SAVOR

You will savor the stories of the struggles, musings, and triumphs of imperfect people like us who are journeying into a deeper relationship with Jesus. You will get a taste of ancient reality as it touches our fast-paced culture. And these bites of life will help to guide, challenge, and focus you.

EXPERIENCE

Faith Café also offers statistics to investigate, books to read, video clips to watch, Web sites to peruse, and thoughts to ponder. The discussions of our society today will provoke groups to enter and experience lessons together. You'll create community and in doing so, learn more about yourself.

WALK

As we examine society's trends and scrutinize Christianity's core beliefs, we choose not to leave it there. We offer suggestions to walk out with the truth you've explored and straightforward strategies for declaring doctrine daily to those around you. Actions such as writing letters, serving meals, or visiting hospitals will allow you to take your faith and share the delight with desperate people.

Every session includes an invitation to experience the truth you're studying on a regular basis. Spiritual disciplines such as intercession, silence, worship, study, and journaling help move you toward transformation. Your heavenly Father can guide and change you as you evaluate your habits and lifestyle.

You are invited to taste and see, to drink and be refreshed. By reflecting and exploring, by examining and investigating, by meditating and applying, you just might discover a way to know God more and to get closer to the person he created you to be. We have no doubt you'll be glad you decided to sit, sip, and talk about life at Faith Café.

A Word for Leaders

Thanks to cell phones and the Internet, communication has never been easier, yet many people suffer from spiritual loneliness. But what if a small group created real community? What if the group's members confessed their worries, hurts, and fears in an environment where hope stays alive? What if friends sat beside friends seeking ways to develop deep, real, alive relationships with their maker? What if people joined together and began a journey of Christian spiritual formation?

Faith Café curriculum was designed for the person seeking this kind of experience. Real growth with real community. Authentic souls seeking to serve others.

Paul encouraged the church at Ephesus saying, "Then we will no longer be infants, tossed back and forth by the waves, and blown here and there by every wind of teaching. . . . Instead, speaking the truth in love, we will in all things grow up into him who is the Head, that is, Christ" (Ephesians 4:14, 15). Just like the Ephesians, we were never meant to receive Christ's salvation and then sit back and do nothing. We were meant to know Jesus and, as a result of getting to know him, to be changed. We believe that Faith Café will help you and your group to grow up in Christ together.

FAITH CAFÉ FEATURES

Faith Café has been designed with leaders in mind. Though we've called this a Leader's Guide, we know that you will want to be a part of this group, not just a face on the other side of a podium. To that end, we provide you with tools to facilitate honest connections and encourage lively, thoughtful discussions. Here's some of what you'll find useful in the five parts that make up each Faith Café episode: ENTER, DRINK, SAVOR, EXPERIENCE, and WALK.

Quotes to think about

Especially in the ENTER section, but also in other parts of each episode, quotes are provided from a variety of writers, performers, and thinkers. In the **Consider it** box, you'll find a quotation that was selected in particular to allow the group to reflect on an aspect of that episode's message or to engage in debate about a meaningful topic.

Scripture support

Though each episode in your leader's guide handily contains all the text that exists in the participant's guide, we've also added some material to be beneficial to you as you walk others through the Bible passages. In GO DEEPER, you'll find insightful information that could help answer questions about or provide context for that episode's Scripture. This section may also contain discussion questions to help you and the members of your group flesh out the message in God's Word.

Facilitating ideas

Besides the Scripture supporting information, each episode is packed with illustrations, activities, media elements, and discussion options that will help to engage every sort of learning style. A **Look into it** box offers

Web sites, books, and other suggestions for further research. And there are no rigid rules or regulations in Faith Café: you may feel free to pick and choose from among the offerings, use none, or use them all!

Adaptable design
We've provided you with some fuel and flavor, but the particular experience is yours to create. Faith Café curriculum is written in a way that allows you to adapt the episode to your own group's unique tastes. Maybe you'll want to start with a bite of life from the SAVOR section one week, and end with a refreshing DRINK from the living Word the next. Or maybe you'll want to follow the order on the page. You and your group can decide what best suits your appetite.

Strategies for service
We don't want your Faith Café experience to end inside the walls of your meeting room. We provide you with simple actions and strategies for taking what you've learned to go—hoping you will make a difference in your community each week and by doing so, stretch and grow in your faith. Spiritual disciplines are also suggested, offering each group member yet another way to care for their souls throughout the week.

SETTING THE SCENE
You may be wondering, *OK, I've got the tools, now where do I start?* We believe that creating a certain kind of environment is an important part of this experience. Think about your favorite coffeehouse or café. What descriptive words do you think of? *Inviting. Relaxing. Warm.* Now imagine how you could recreate that setting for your group. It may be as simple as bringing in a couple of lamps for softer lighting, or arranging the seats in a circle so everyone can see each other. What resources does your group have available? Maybe you can find comfortable chairs and cozy couches at your local thrift store. Will you have a large group? Maybe you can use a tall stool to speak from instead of standing. Make it a multi-sensory experience. Have music playing as group members arrive. Don't forget the necessary equipment for playing the Faith Café DVD clips! And finally, think about bringing snacks, drinks, and of course, coffee, to complete the scene. See www.standardpub.com/faithcafe for more ideas on creating a Faith Café space in your church.

It's important to remember that community will happen only in a trusting and authentic atmosphere. This may take a few weeks to cultivate, but know that people are hungry for a place where they can truly be known and know others. Be willing to share your own struggles, doubts, or dreams with the group to demonstrate the importance of honest dialogue. Be sensitive to the questions or pains that others share by taking time to talk through issues and pray, even if it means leaving out a portion of the lesson. Be patient with those who are quiet or shy by giving them time to get comfortable in this new environment.

Finally, pray. Pray that God will bring about dramatic transformation. Pray that he will build relationships that go deep and stand strong. As you can see, Faith Café is more than a topical curriculum that happens once a week. It's a place to create a community that can change lives. If you're interested in designing a space in your church, Faith Café is for you. You're invited to taste and see, to drink and be refreshed. Come on in—everyone is welcome.

A Man and a Nation

SUPPLIES NEEDED

History books and historical pictures

Favorite films on DVD (ask participants)

White board or chalkboard

Dry-erase markers or chalk

Faith Café DVD

ENTER

Have you ever invited friends over to join you in watching one of your favorite old movies? This week, we invite you to watch a classic. It is fascinating non-fiction. It involves a Top Ten list, but nothing like most modern Top Ten lists. We'll meet a man you will want to get to know. We'll see him fail, struggle, and eventually succeed. And we'll watch an entire nation follow this hero, Moses, as he is led by God.

As we watch, we may notice a bit of ourselves.

As Moses hears from God, we'll hear much of why our own desires get in God's way and how trusting God may be the best choice after all.

So grab your popcorn and your favorite soft drink. Travel with us into ancient history and prepare to find out a lot about yourself while we're there.

Show history books or pictures of historical events to the group. Take some time to let everyone discuss what these scenes or stories bring to mind. Emphasize how historical events shape human life. Each one has the potential to guide the world in ways it wasn't previously going. Invite the participants to consider how the giving of the Ten Commandments to Moses impacted

the world and to keep those thoughts in mind as you begin this study together.

It's film festival time at Faith Café. Play back some of your all-time favorite movies in your mind right now. Consider what made the plots compelling. Consider the plights of the heroes and heroines. Then ask yourself these questions:

- What is it about these films that intrigue me?
- What movie heroes do I relate to most? Why?
- How have these movie heroes impacted me and my dreams?
- What could I do in my life that would really be considered heroic?
- If a movie were made of my life as it stands today, what would the plot be?

Consider bringing a favorite classic film with you to this session and playing a clip for the group. Or, before the group meets, invite members to bring their favorite DVDs with them. You could then play a few clips for the group and discuss what makes these movies so memorable.

Consider it

"This thing of being a hero, about the main thing to it is to know when to die."

—Will Rogers, humorist

Have the group discuss what this quote means. Can people think of influential figures who might have been remembered more as heroes if they had died earlier than what they did? What are the standards for attaining hero status these days? Does the group think these standards are good ones?

DRINK

Before reading today's Scripture with participants, write the name Moses on the board. Use each letter of his name to write words that describe what participants know about him. Ask:

- *What comes to your mind when you hear the name Moses?*
- *What do you know about his life?*

Add words like these if they aren't included: man, mystery, miracles, obedience, objections, orders, sin, safety, enemies, eyes, evil, surrender, submission.

Invite your group to listen to the reading of a portion from Stephen's sermon in Acts 7, where he gave a history lesson about the nation of Israel. See the GO DEEPER section where his more extended comments reveal some more important things about Moses. You may wish to read parts of the Scripture presented there first.

This is the same Moses whom they had rejected with the words, "Who made you ruler and judge?" He was sent to be their ruler and deliverer by God himself, through the angel who appeared to him in the bush. He led them out of Egypt and did wonders and miraculous signs in Egypt, at the Red Sea and for forty years in the desert. This is that Moses who told the Israelites, "God will send you a prophet like me from your own people." He was in the assembly in the desert, with the angel who spoke to him on Mount Sinai, and with our fathers; and he received living words to pass on to us.

—Acts 7:35-38

Moses: a man who shaped history. Like other stars in biblical drama, the script of Moses' life contains mystery, miracles, mistakes, words from God, and surprising responses. His story has a strange beginning, seasons of silent training, and a unique journey.

Moses: a baby whose life was spared. He grew to be an Israelite serving a nation that sought to kill him. He was a chosen man, whose zealous desire for change

pushed him away for forty years. A doubtful man, who struggled to believe he was the one that God had chosen to speak to a nation. A startled runaway, who heard from God and obeyed his instructions.

Moses: the name means "drawn out of the water." As a baby, he had been drawn out of a river. As a leader, he was used by God to draw a nation out of bondage.

Moses: a shadow of someone to come. Another prophet would arrive from the Jewish people, to lead not only them, but all humankind from the bondage of sin. Yet he would also face rejection.

Can miracles result from the rescue of a baby? Can a simple man enter an evil empire and rescue an entire people? Can God speak to us? If he does, will we listen?

GO DEEPER

We can learn a lot about the Ten Commandments by listening to a sermon in the New Testament preached by Stephen in Acts 7. He proclaimed truth that directly contradicted his audience's actions. He voiced a history lesson and left them little room for argument. Their final response was to kill him for disrupting their religious assumptions. Read some more of Stephen's speech:

At that time Moses was born, and he was no ordinary child. For three months he was cared for in his father's house. When he was placed outside, Pharaoh's daughter took him and brought him up as her own son. Moses was educated in all the wisdom of the Egyptians and was powerful in speech and action.

When Moses was forty years old, he decided to visit his fellow Israelites. He saw one of them being mistreated by an Egyptian, so he went to his defense and avenged him by killing the Egyptian. Moses thought that his own people would realize that God was using him to rescue them, but they did not. The next day Moses came upon two Israelites who were fighting. He tried to reconcile them by saying, "Men, you are brothers; why do you want to hurt each other?"

But the man who was mistreating the other pushed Moses aside and said, "Who made you ruler and judge over us? Do you want to kill me as you killed the Egyptian yesterday?" When Moses heard this, he fled to Midian, where he settled as a foreigner and had two sons.

After forty years had passed, an angel appeared to Moses in the flames of a burning bush in the desert near Mount Sinai. When he saw this, he was amazed at the sight. As he went over to look more closely, he heard the Lord's voice: "I am the God of your fathers, the God of Abraham, Isaac and Jacob." Moses trembled with fear and did not dare to look.

Then the Lord said to him, "Take off your sandals; the place where you are standing is holy ground. I have indeed seen the oppression of my people in Egypt. I have heard their groaning and have come down to set them free. Now come, I will send you back to Egypt." (Acts 7:20-34)

Stephen gave Moses credit for what God was doing in the early church. To mention Moses and connect him (someone the audience adored) to the new followers of Christ (people the audience despised) brought serious tension to the atmosphere.

Stephen, described as a man full of grace and power, had just been selected as a servant to meet the needs of the church's poor. Accepting the responsibility, Stephen served. But he was also an outspoken and bold man. In his fascinating sermon, he summarized the historical foundation of Jewish beliefs and connected Jewish history to the new Christian church. The result? Stephen was stoned to death, but the truth was declared.

Where does that leave us? Stephen's sermon—and his willingness to risk everything—testifies that as we study Moses and the Ten Commandments, we aren't just studying history. We are opening ourselves up to truth others died to proclaim.

———————●———————

Play the Episode 27 (Lesson 1) clip from the Faith Café DVD. Discuss the "God as Grandfather" sketch performed by actor Curt Cloninger. Ask the following questions:

- *How do aspects of this comic sketch resemble the way you sometimes see God?*
- *How could seeing God in this manner harm your faith?*
- *Do you believe this is a popular view of God? Why or why not?*
- *What quote or statement from this clip was most powerful for you? Why?*

SAVOR

Remember for any section that has some reading, it's always a good idea to invite participants to share in this activity.

Jack was born in 1919 into a Southern culture steeped in racism. He reacted by fighting back, developing a reputation as a brawler. Even on his college campus in southern California he was considered to be a thug. But on that same campus he met a minister named Karl Downs whose sermons challenged him. A black man like Jack, Downs helped Jack see that Christianity did not require acceptance of racism, but supplied a better way of fighting it than through violence.

By 1945, Jack had become convinced that God had an important task for him to accomplish. He was unclear of what that was until he was offered a job in a field that had barred African Americans. The offer came from a man who told Jack that he was looking for an employee "with guts enough not to fight back." The man also handed Jack a copy of a book by Giovanni Papini called *The Life of Christ*, and he reminded him of Jesus' command to turn the other cheek when wronged. Jack accepted the job. During his ten years of employment, he endured racist remarks, death threats, and was refused hotel accommodations when traveling on company business. But Jack's faith helped him keep his anger in check. This faithful hero is known today as the man who broke baseball's color barrier. Jack Roosevelt "Jackie" Robinson is one of the most famous of all sports heroes. But he was more than a baseball player. He was a man called on a mission from a God who empowered and sustained him.

List these words on the board for the participants to see:

- *Rescued*
- *Raised*
- *Rejected*
- *Rewarded*

With the group, look back through today's Scripture and talk about the significance of God's rescuing Moses as a child from death, having him be raised by a nation he would one day battle, Moses' own efforts to change the world leading to rejection, and God's ultimate rewarding of his obedience. Give participants time to talk about their own lives as well as the ways their efforts to solve problems have sometimes gotten in the way of God's long-term plan.

EXPERIENCE

George Clymer was apprenticed to his paternal uncle in preparation for a career as a merchant. Lyman Hall was a supply preacher and teacher. Button Gwinnett farmed a Georgia plantation. These ordinary men and fifty-three others stood upon their convictions and signed the Declaration of Independence. What extraordinary task may you be called to perform?

Look into it

- Earl Creps, *Off-Road Disciplines: Spiritual Disciplines of Missional Leaders*
- Bill Hybels, *Engraved on Your Heart: Living the Ten Commandments Day by Day*
- www.oldtestamentstudies.net/

WALK

The words given to Moses for the purpose of changing a nation ultimately changed the world.

In our life's walk, how can we influence our own country? How can we help guide a nation and a world down better paths? Is it possible?

At Faith Café, we believe it is. We believe we are shaping this world's future. Our plan is to shape it in obedience to our heavenly Father.

This week, take time to live the truth by preparing to obey the God who brings freedom. Rather than doing anything too quickly and reacting incorrectly, as Moses often did, hide away with God.

Dedicate your ordinary life to be a part of God's extraordinary plan this week:

- Listen. Read Acts 7:20-38 again.
- Journal your thoughts, dreams, ideas, hopes, and possibilities.
- Leave your notes alone for a while and go spend time with God.
- Each day ask God to use you as a world changer, living in ways that help to lead people out of whatever is holding them back.

This week's spiritual discipline is dying:

As we prepare to study the Ten Commandments, what is the best method of training? We need to die. Take time to focus on the discipline of personal dying. As Christians, we must learn how to die to ourselves and to our prideful, selfish motives. Give all to God and live stronger than ever.

NOTES

The Word Was God

SUPPLIES NEEDED

White board or chalkboard
Dry-erase marker or chalk
Paper and pens or pencils
Faith Café DVD

ENTER

Are you ready for this? At Faith Café today, we'll be starting to discuss the Ten Commandments. How do you feel about that? Do you think you've heard it all before? Do you wonder if these commands really matter anymore? Are you afraid the times of study are going to be a guilt trip, reminding you of how you have failed to meet God's standards?

Before we listen to God's commands voiced to Moses long ago, let's make sure we're ready by getting on the same page. You may want to pray: *God, help me to approach your words in the right frame of mind and to focus on what you want me to learn.*

Let's think a little more about the process of and need for preparation. Ask yourself:

- How do you prepare for a business trip or a vacation?
- What are some ways you have prepared for taking a test?
- What routine have you gone through in preparing for a nice date?
- How would you recommend that a candidate prepare for a job interview?
- Think about a time when you wished you had been more prepared.

"If I had six hours to chop down a tree, I'd spend the first hour sharpening the ax."

—Abraham Lincoln

Take a moment to discuss what preparations might need to be made before studying the Ten Commandments. Make two columns on the board. At the top of one write GET RID OF, *and on the other write* GET HOLD OF. *Have the participants contribute ideas for each column, talking about what issues, ideas, beliefs we need to get rid of or get hold of as we begin to study the Ten Commandments.*

Consider it

"America, where thanks to Congress, there are forty million laws to enforce the Ten Commandments."

—Anatole France, French author

Take some time to discuss the Consider it *quote. Ask these questions:*

- *Do you think this quote rings true? Why or why not?*
- *Why do you think we spend so much time spelling out ways to obey the Ten Commandments?*
- *Do you think it's a good idea to analyze God's Word? What problems do you experience or see others going through in studying God's Word? What benefits do you or others gain?*

DRINK

In the beginning was the Word, and the Word was with God, and the Word was God. He was with God in the beginning.

Through him all things were made; without him nothing was made that has been made. In him was life, and that life was the light of men. The light shines in the darkness, but the darkness has not understood it.

—John 1:1-5

John wrote his Gospel decades after Matthew, Mark, and Luke wrote theirs. So why did the church need another account of Jesus' life? We get a clue from this unique beginning of John. The apostle was battling false ideas about the message God had for them. He went back to the start of time to get the church on the same page.

GO DEEPER

John's Gospel opens in a unique way: with a proclamation declaring historical truth, letting readers know from the beginning the view that all remaining verses will hold. Let's look closely at what these verses have to say to us.

Time—"In the beginning . . ." John's Gospel declares. These words refer to the start of the new season, the coming of the Messiah. But they also refer to the beginning of time, of life. The Gospel of John reveals an amazing, mind-bending reality: "The news you read here started before life as we know it."

Word—John calls this truth "the Word" and explains several things about it: time (in the beginning), location (with God), and person (God). And notice this: all things were made by this Word and through this Word, without it, nothing was made.

Life—The Word (this person of God who was from the beginning) contained an interesting element. It was not a dead thing, something in the past to be forgotten. It contained life—vibrant, light infused life. This life is described as "the light of men." It is a force that repels darkness.

Now—What does this mean for us? Just as John hoped his readers would embrace the truth, we can have finding the truth be a goal for our study of Moses and the Ten Commandments.

These verses of John remind us of what came before and after Moses, a nation's journey, and ten rules on a rock. God was, is, and forever shall be. Knowing, believing, and living that truth allows us to see more than some old stones giving us ten old rules that no longer apply to our lives. Through studying the Word, we are given the opportunity to learn more about finding and living that life that is the "light of men."

Here are some other verses that reveal to us the importance and character of the Word of God:

Do everything without complaining or arguing, so that you may become blameless and pure, children of God without fault in a crooked and depraved generation, in which you shine like stars in the universe as you hold out the word of life—in order that I may boast on the day of Christ that I did not run or labor for nothing.

—Philippians 2:14-16

Let the word of Christ dwell in you richly as you teach and admonish one another with all wisdom, and as you sing psalms, hymns and spiritual songs with gratitude in your hearts to God.

—Colossians 3:16

In fact, everyone who wants to live a godly life in Christ Jesus will be persecuted, while evil men and impostors will go from bad to worse, deceiving and being deceived. But as for you, continue in what you have learned and have become convinced of, because you know those from whom you learned it, and how from infancy you have known the holy Scriptures, which are able to make you wise for salvation through faith in Christ Jesus. All Scripture is God-breathed and is useful for teaching, rebuking, correcting and training in righteousness, so that the man of God may be thoroughly equipped for every good work.

—2 Timothy 3:12-17

For the word of God is living and active. Sharper than any double-edged sword, it penetrates even to dividing soul and spirit, joints and marrow; it judges the thoughts and attitudes of the heart.

—Hebrews 4:12

He chose to give us birth through the word of truth, that we might be a kind of firstfruits of all he created.

—James 1:18

Now that you have purified yourselves by obeying the truth so that you have sincere love for your brothers, love one another deeply, from the heart. For you have been born again, not of perishable seed, but of imperishable, through the living and enduring word of God. For,
     "All men are like grass,
       and all their glory is like the flowers of
         the field;
     the grass withers and the flowers fall,
       but the word of the Lord stands forever."
And this is the word that was preached to you.

—1 Peter 1:22-25

⬤

SAVOR

Tom and Karen felt better when they picked Rick up from Vacation Bible School. They were pleased to see a huge smile on his face. Karen said, "Look—he's happy. He acts like he doesn't want to leave."

That was new for Tom and Karen. Seeing Rick smile, seeing him happy with other children his age and willing to be somewhere away from his mom and dad: that was all new. They couldn't remember when Rick had seemed this happy outside of his own room. They wanted to know why.

Rick jumped into their Suburban, waved good-bye to two other boys, and sat down to finish off his peanut M&Ms. Rick's parents both wanted to know every detail.

Rick interrupted the silence. "Wanna know what I learned today?" he asked.

Karen said, "Yes, Rick. Tell us all about it."

During the next ten minutes, their drive home was different from previous rides. They had feared Rick would hate being at a church event since it was so new to him. But as he told them what he learned about God, Jesus, and himself, Karen and Tom heard what was almost like a sermon: God created Rick in his own image; God loved Rick so much that Jesus died for him, a little boy who thought most people would never like him; laws and rules are for our protection, not silly mandates to make life boring; and if Rick did something wrong, God would forgive him even though God did not like what he had done. Rick talked and talked. Rapidly he summarized a day that would change his life forever.

Tom glanced at the clock while Rick told about Jesus' dying on the cross and coming back to life. Karen held back tears as she thought about Grandmamma teaching her all those Bible stories before she grew up and became "too smart" to believe them anymore. Karen wanted to believe again. Rick sounded as if he believed them. As he talked, the stories did not sound like fairy tales.

Rick said, "Can I go back tomorrow?"

As Tom pulled into their two-car garage, Karen said, "Yes, Rick. If you want to, I'll take you."

Ask these questions:
- *Why was Rick so happy?*
- *What portions of God's story make you feel happy?*
- *Why do you think people sometimes think that God's Word is like a bunch of fairy tales? Have you ever felt this way? Describe that experience.*
- *Did you find it easier to believe in God and stories from the Bible when you were a child? Why or why not?*
- *What aspects of being an adult serve as obstacles to belief?*

Pass out paper and pens or pencils and invite the participants to add another paragraph to the story. What conversation might have happened later between Karen and Tom? Ask people to share their writing if they wish. Conclude the time with prayer, asking God to help us not let things in our lives take the place of the truth.

EXPERIENCE

The theological differences between Christianity and Islam are numerous and complex. But there exists a simple difference at the core. Christians are taught to see God as a loving Father. He is a relationship God. Muslim teaching focuses upon the justice of God. He is a lawmaking, judging God.

At risk of oversimplifying, what would you expect to be the results of starting out with one view or the other? How would beginning with a God of love or a God of justice affect families? relationships? civil law? conduct between nations? What has been your view of God, and how has that made a difference in your life?

Play the Episode 28 (Lesson 2) clip from the Faith Café DVD. Conclude with the following questions:
- *What was the point of this excerpt?*
- *In what areas of your life do you most often seek direction?*
- *How important is it to have direction in your spiritual life? Why?*
- *What thoughts does this clip bring to mind about your spiritual life?*

Look into it
- Bonnie Bruno, *When God Steps In: Stories of Everyday Grace*
- R.C. Sproul, *Knowing Scripture*
- www.annegrahamlotz.com
- www.desiringgod.org

WALK

To get ready for a study of the Ten Commandments, we let the apostle John prepare us by helping us understand what God's message is. The message of God is more than a list of rules to live by. The Word is a person, Jesus Christ. God's message walked on this earth and sought a relationship with human beings. He still does.

How can we live in a way that acknowledges that, in John's words, "The law was given through Moses; grace and truth came through Jesus Christ"(John 1:17)? How does knowing that God is in the relationship business rather than in law enforcement keep us humble and gracious to those we must deal with on a daily basis?

"Most of us think about how we can change culture. Sacred realism gives culture a chance to change us."

—Earl Creps, *Off-Road Disciplines*

"In the beginning was the Word." What do those words mean to you? To your neighbors? To walk in the truth this week, think about what it means to welcome God into your life. Try this:

- Make a list of ways you desire to see the Light (Jesus) shine through your words, attitudes, and actions.
- Consider speaking to those you normally ignore. Smile at sad faces even though you know they won't smile back.

This week's spiritual discipline is truth:
Invest some thought this week in how acknowledging the reality of life can help you grow stronger in Christ. Talk through your ideas with someone else. Be willing to practice being truthful by admitting to someone when you make a mistake instead of hiding or trying to act as if you are a perfect Christian.

NOTES

Put God First

SUPPLIES NEEDED

Top Ten lists from the Web or hard copies

Dry-erase marker or chalk

Paper and pens or pencils

Faith Café DVD

"Center" by Matt Redman and Charlie Hall, from *Flying into Daybreak*

ENTER

Top Ten lists. We've seen a lot of them: books, music, movies, sports teams, restaurants, politicians, athletes, singers, and actors. We could all create some type of Top Ten list—maybe ten resolutions to start a new year or ten commitments to end our old ways. Letterman offers his list; ESPN offers its own.

But what about God? If he voiced his list of Top Ten Commandments, what would they be?

In Exodus we read that God spoke to Moses and gave us what we label the Ten Commandments. The entire Bible reveals God's rules, instructions, and warnings. But the Ten Commandments sum them all up. We can use a variety of words to describe them, but we cannot overemphasize their importance.

Before the session or during it (if you have Internet access available) peruse a few Web sites that offer Top Ten lists. (Check the appropriateness of the listed sites before you meet as sites change frequently.)
www.merriam-webster.com/info/06words.htm
www.ssa.gov/OACT/babynames/
www.soyouwanna.com/site/features/topten.html
www.alternet.org/story/30157/ (this site is a few years out of date, but some of the lists are still interesting)

(If you don't have Internet access during the session, print out a few of the lists and make copies for each member that you can pass out at the meeting.)

Discuss with the group what kinds of Top Ten lists are interesting to them. Why are Top Ten lists interesting to people in general? Make up your own Top Ten lists and write them on the board: Top Ten Coffee Orders, Top Ten Date Nights, Top Ten Breakfast Pastries. Talk about the different factors that put an item at the top of a list: popularity, frequency of use, quality, etc.

Look around. Think of the lists that come to mind. A coffee shop menu . . . the roster of members of your group . . . the things you need to get done when you leave this place. What puts something on the top of your lists? Consider these questions:

- Think of all the possessions in your house. Which ones are dearest to you and why?

- Think of all of the people who play a part in your life. Who is at or near the top of that list? Why?

- Think of all the activities you participate in during a typical week. What is at the top of the list? Why?

- List some causes or ideas in which you deeply believe. What is at the top of that list? Why?

Consider it

"Government's first duty and highest obligation is public safety."

—Arnold Schwarzenegger

"First things first, second things never."

—Shirley Conran, novelist

Ask the group:

- *Do you agree or disagree with the quote from Governor Schwarzenegger? Why or why not?*
- *How can ideas about what is most important affect the actions of a government?*
- *What do you think is meant by the second quote? What relationship might exist between these two quotes?*
- *How do your views about what is most important shape how you live your life?*

DRINK

I am the LORD your God, who brought you out of Egypt, out of the land of slavery. You shall have no other gods before me.

—Exodus 20:2, 3

The first command is not only first in sequence, but also first in importance. Only by obeying it can we possibly obey the others. This command lays the foundation for the rest. God reminded the Israelites that he had the authority to make this demand because of who he was and what he had done for them. The same is true for us today. Allegiance to God must be our first priority because he has provided everything we have.

GO DEEPER

Let's set the scene for the giving of the Ten Commandments. Read the following passage from Exodus 19:16-20; 20:1-3:

On the morning of the third day there was thunder and lightning, with a thick cloud over the mountain, and a very loud trumpet blast. Everyone in the camp trembled. Then Moses led the people out of the camp to meet with God, and they stood at the foot of the mountain. Mount Sinai was covered with smoke, because the LORD descended on it in fire. The smoke billowed up from it like smoke from a furnace, the whole mountain trembled violently, and the sound of the trumpet grew louder and louder. Then Moses spoke and the voice of God answered him.

The LORD descended to the top of Mount Sinai and called Moses to the top of the mountain. So Moses went up. . . . And God spoke all these words:

"I am the LORD your God, who brought you out of Egypt, out of the land of slavery. You shall have no other gods before me."

The scene related here might seem strange or even scary. It reminds us that although God loves us and wants to communicate with us, God is not just a buddy next door. He is our maker, our master, and our ruler.

As we seek to live in this self-centered, feelings-centered, quick-fix world, God's laws offer a needed revelation of practical holiness and committed love. God wanted a new life for his people. Egypt—a place packed with false gods, idols, and sin—had reflected the opposite of God's desires. The first command may not at first glance seem too strange to our modern ears: God proclaiming his identity and demanding his people's allegiance. But this was a time when the people in power, the rulers of the lands, worshiped many gods. This was the norm. The very fact that God felt it necessary to make this command points to this. And some may even wish to interpret this statement to mean something along the lines of "You may have other gods, but I am to be first." However, this is not what is meant here. God is saying something new, something outstanding: "Have no other gods, not any in my presence—

before me, behind me, above me, below me." This is emphasized by the next commandment, which clearly demonstrates that God wants his people to worship *only* him.

The first command is not only first in sequence, but also first because only through obeying it can we possibly obey the others. This command lays the foundation for the rest. It reminds us of who God is and what he has done for us. Thus, we are called to do what we ought for him.

But the Old Testament reveals how Israel continually rebelled against this command and went back to their old ways. Something so crucial and so simple, yet they just couldn't stick with it. Sound like anyone you know?

 Play the Episode 29 (Lesson 3) clip from the Faith Café DVD, which features musical artist Marcus Cole sharing about writing worship songs. After viewing it, ask the following questions as you focus on putting God first:

- *What does worship have to do with the first commandment?*
- *How can using your talents keep you connected to and focused on God?*
- *How do you think God speaks to us today? Do you think he can speak through music?*
- *When you hear people say that they feel God is speaking through them, does that make sense to you? Why or why not?*

SAVOR

Mark sat down for dinner at home.

Leftovers from lunch were just what he needed. He felt relaxed. The pressure at work had not diminished, but he was learning a lot from his accountability group since he had started attending a church in his new town.

Sitting at his small table, glancing out the window to his left and then to the television straight ahead, he clicked the channel changer. The news got his attention.

Another protest, he thought. *Always something.* As Mark listened, he realized this debate highlighted the subject that was discussed in last week's small-group meeting: the Ten Commandments.

Anger came through as the reporter asked a protester why he was standing for a cause he could not control. His answer caused Mark to stop eating for a moment: "To remove the Ten Commandments from schools and public places is to remove the foundation from our nation. We must take a stand against those who seek only to be politically correct. I am standing up for God, not man." The reporter looked into the camera and gave an update on the debate.

Mark remembered that the small-group study had barely made it past the first commandment. He wanted to think it over once more. Opening his Bible and rereading Exodus 20:1-3, Mark felt as if God were talking directly to him.

Mark noticed the notes he'd written near that passage. As his group had discussed and debated, he had taken time to critique his own gods, his own substitutes, his own idols. His comment to the group was still written down: "We often act like it's OK for God to be just a part of our lives. That is wrong. He is to be everything. If not, what takes priority over him becomes a god in place of him."

He looked up at the TV screen and thought, *How am I doing with the list I wrote about possible "gods" in my life? What must I do to keep those people, positions, and desires in their proper places? While others debate about keeping the Ten Commandments on display, am I living in obedience to those commands so others can see more of God in my life?*

Mark suddenly had a deep, fresh longing to live for, submit to, and honor God. Before finishing his dinner, he stopped to pray: *God, let this small moment of realization make me different. Help me love you more. Protect me from letting anything come between you and me. Amen.*

Discuss how Mark clued in to what was on the channel in front of him and made a connection with what was happening in his spiritual life. Ask:
- *How do you select what spiritual, mental, emotional, and physical "channels" play in your life? Are you intentional about them, or do you just let life happen to you as you respond spontaneously?*
- *What are some things that threaten to become or already are "gods" in your life? (e.g., career,*

money, pleasure, image, and family)

- *What about the question Mark asked himself: "Am I living in obedience to those commands so others can see more of God in my life?" What would your answer be?*

EXPERIENCE

According to research done by the Barna Group, 71% of Americans believe in an all-powerful, all-knowing, perfect creator of the universe who rules the world today. Yet 61% believe gambling is morally acceptable; 60% believe living with someone outside of marriage is OK; and 75% say they are open to "alternative moral views." What do those statistics say to you?

Look into it

- Joel Warne, *Soul Craving*
- Erwin Lutzer, *Christ Among Other Gods*
- The Barna Group, www.barna.org/
- The List Universe, www.listverse.com/

Consider playing the song "Center" by Matt Redman and Charlie Hall during your time together (Charlie Hall, Flying into Daybreak, Sparrow, 2006). After the song, ask group members to comment on how this song fits today's topic. You may want to use these questions to focus the discussion:

- *Why is it so difficult to keep Christ at the center of our lives?*
- *What is the difference between having God as a part of your life and having God as the center of your life?*

WALK

This week, before moving beyond yourself and your group, evaluate where you stand with God, and how you are doing in avoiding setting up other gods in your life.

Is God what really matters most to you? Is God truly God for you? Does what you say you believe about God show in how you live the rest of your life? If not, take time to ask him to become your only God. Look for the dark corners in which you find it easier to follow the crowd rather than to place God on the throne of your life. Welcome him to that place. To help

with this, spend time praying and journaling ways to let this wonderful reality continue in your life.

"An unexamined life is not worth living."

—Socrates

Consider how well you put God first in all that you think and do this week:

- Set aside time to review and critique your obedience to the first commandment.
- Think through your personal perspectives on important topics. How are those perspectives informed by what you believe about God?
- Read God's Word and books by various Christian authors on social and moral issues, Let your reading challenge your thinking.

This week's spiritual discipline is perspective: We *live* life based on how we see life. This week, examine your point of view (POV). Moses and the Israelites needed a shift in POV; God gave them the Ten Commandments to help them change. Assess your POV; be refreshed, and be intentional about how you live and think.

If time allows, try this exercise to help the group to start thinking about POV. Read the following quote and ask the questions that follow.

"We are supposedly a country at war, but we're all going about watching American Idol and having not all that different a time than if we weren't at war. I observe the weird juxtaposition of reading the newspaper and then tuning in to American Idol and getting really upset when Constantine gets voted off and then wondering where my head was at. But in a way, that's also the salvation of the country, our level of optimism."

—*Paul Weitz, American filmmaker*

- *What do you think about what Paul Weitz says in this quote?*
- *What does this say about the perspective of most Americans? Is it a positive or a negative attribute of our nation?*

What Else Am I Worshiping?

SUPPLIES NEEDED

Ads from magazines, newspapers, or the Internet

White board or chalkboard

Dry-erase marker or chalk

Faith Café DVD

Paper and pens or pencils

ENTER

Have you ever allowed someone else's possessions to make you a little envious? Maybe you've even said, "But those people have so much more." Maybe you've thought, *I want what they have.* Though the words seem immature, even childish, when we read them on paper, haven't most of us had these thoughts at some time?

What are some things that feed your envy? Take a moment to recall some advertisements that you have seen recently. What messages were they trying to get you to believe? What were they trying to get you to do or feel? Think of one ad that was particularly successful in making you want something you didn't have.

Imagine that God is an advertiser here at Faith Café. Take a moment and hear his message to you. How does it differ from the lures of our commercial culture?

Bring a few ads to your meeting. Discuss the questions above and talk about how the things or scenes presented in the ads may cause us to become envious. Be sensitive in your discussion of the different financial backgrounds that may be represented in your group.

Talk about how these ads may not affect us in obvious ways ("I'm going to go buy that new Toyota now."), but still affect us all the same ("My car is looking kind of worn. I'll never be able to save enough to get a new one. Poor me."). Talk about how the lifestyle represented in these ads might seem to people in various other countries, particularly those in great need.

After the discussion you may want to begin the session in prayer, asking God to draw our attention to the idols we may have in our lives and to heal us of the temptation always to lust for more.

Pagans in ancient days made idols of wood and metal that they bowed down to and worshiped. It's not like that today. Or is it? Think about some things that may be idols in your own life:

- If you knew that your house would burn down this evening, what one thing would you take out of it today?

- Think of one person who means more to you than anyone else in this world. What was the last fight you had with that person? Was the cause of that fight something of temporal or of eternal value?

- What is the biggest time-waster in your life?

Consider it

"'Tis mad idolatry to make the service greater than the god."

—William Shakespeare, *Troilus and Cressida*

Ask the group:
- *What does this quote say to you?*
- *Are you ever guilty of showing more devotion to something than it is worth?*
- *What about in the church? Have you ever thought that it seems that the "service" is greater than the God who is meant to be the center of the worship?*

You could also make two columns on the board: The God and The Service. Under each heading have participants contribute ideas for activities that take up our time in a normal week that are done especially for God or especially for "the service." Suggest that "service" in this context could mean the church service itself or a particular ministry or just our daily tasks of life—taking care of our families and loved ones.

DRINK

You shall not make for yourself an idol in the form of anything in heaven above or on the earth beneath or in the waters below. You shall not bow down to them or worship them; for I, the LORD your God, am a jealous God, punishing the children for the sin of the fathers to the third and fourth generation of those who hate me, but showing love to a thousand generations of those who love me and keep my commandments.

—Exodus 20:4-6

When we think of idols today, we do not usually think of statues we worship. We use the term to describe people that we look up to—often movie, TV, or sports personalities. How do we show our devotion to these idols? We try to *be* them.

This prohibition of idols in the Ten Commandments contains a warning of punishment. God is going to punish the children and grandchildren and great-grandchildren of idolaters. How will that happen? How is that fair?

The problem with idols (whether they be Hollywood stars or statuettes) is that we become what and whom we worship. The psalmist warns against idols, not only because they are powerless to truly help us, but because "those who make them will be like them, and so will all who trust in them" (Psalm 135:18).

When we try to be like anyone other than Christ, we fall into a trap and lead following generations into that same snare.

GO DEEPER

Read the following words from Philip Yancey's book *The Bible Jesus Read* (Zondervan, 1999, p. 93) to the class. It will help set the mood for our discussion on the Ten Commandments:

When God makes a list of commandments, Love takes first place, the basis for his whole relationship with humanity. God meets in a tent and discusses policy, as a man speaks to a friend. He listens, and he argues back. God also feels pain. When jilted, God suffers like any wounded lover. He makes threats, and then backs down from them. He negotiates and signs contracts.

This last fact, above all, separated the Hebrews from their neighbors. Even the haughty Egyptians lived in fear of their capricious gods. The Canaanites sacrificed children to appease their unpredictable gods. But the God of the Hebrews proved willing to sign a contract detailing exactly what he expected from his people, and what he promised in return.

Except for Orthodox Jews, not many people today devote time to the legal code recorded in Exodus, Leviticus, and Deuteronomy. Yet, as Deuteronomy shows most clearly, these laws simply set the boundaries of a vastly unequal relationship: between an awesome, holy God and an ordinary people prone to failure and rebellion.

Ask these questions:
- What do Yancey's comments say to us today?
- When we think of the Ten Commandments, do we think of love, or judgment? Why?
- Do you think your view is accurate? How?

- How are we different from the Israelites? How are we similar?

Say these words from Exodus 20:4-6 from *The Message* aloud:

No carved gods of any size, shape, or form of anything whatever, whether of things that fly or walk or swim. Don't bow down to them and don't serve them because *I* am GOD, your God, and I'm a most jealous God, punishing the children for any sins their parents pass on to them to the third, and yes, even to the fourth generation of those who hate me. But I'm unswervingly loyal to the thousands who love me and keep my commandments.

Can't we again see how God formed the commands as a guide toward practical holiness? God hated the spiritual adultery of idolatry. Matthew Henry described it this way in his commentary:

God looks upon them as haters of him, though they perhaps pretend love to him; he will visit their iniquity; that is, he will very severely punish it, not only as a breach of his law, but as an affront to his majesty, a violation of the covenant, and a blow at the root of all religion.

God has no room for such a breach of the law. His firmness in this command revealed his displeasure. He voiced his order to a nation that had grown up in Egypt, knowing a multitude of gods and goddesses. They carried some of their affinity for and knowledge of other religions with them as they were led out of slavery. However, God refused to let them carry the luggage of idolatry into the Promised Land.

But what about us? Where do we stand regarding such a vivid command? False gods are passed on from generation to generation these days as well. What ones have been passed down to you?

We need to be aware that God's judgments have not departed today, to be replaced by his avoidance or ignorance of our idolatry. He knows. He corrects those who place him beside or beneath other gods. He rebukes disobedience out of love. He knows what improper priorities can do. He warned the nation of Israel. He warns us.

SAVOR

Vicky finally found a parking place. . . . She never felt excited at the mall. Her friends loved shopping and spending so they had met earlier to check out the latest trends and deals and sales, but Vicky had told them she could get there only in time for dinner.

She really didn't want to be there at all. . . .

Since she had arrived a little early, Vicky sat in her car thinking, *Will things always be like this?* Suddenly her mind hit reverse, and Vicky remembered some of the experiences that had left her angry and bitter.

Her parents had spent most of their time in their busy jobs. Vicky, an only child, saw them before going to bed at night and before school in the morning. Rarely did they enjoy time, conversations, or laughter together. Oh, her family had expensive vacations. And they bought Vicky the latest clothes, cars, computers, and anything else they assumed she desired. But Vicky's parents failed to realize she wanted to be with *them*.

For a few years, Vicky liked her role as the lucky girl, but since her parents' divorce and her decision to live on her own, any place that reminds her of them or their lifestyle brings sick feelings. She can still hear her mother and father making their usual comment when they saw people who owned a bigger house or nicer vehicle: "Those people have so much more than we do."

Vicky felt that her parents worshiped the god of things, possessions, and wealth. Counseling had been helping her deal with her feelings, and one day she hoped she would be able to enter a mall without allowing her past to rob her of joy. But tonight? She stayed in her car until her friends called to say they had arrived at the restaurant.

Ask the group these questions:
- *What about Vicky's story stood out to you?*
- *The idols that were passed down to Vicky had poisoned her enjoyment of life. Are there any idols like this in your family tree? What effect have they had on you?*
- *Why do you think some people feel better when they buy things? What would be one activity we could do instead of making a purchase that also might generate good feelings?*

EXPERIENCE

"All men want to be happy, but we make the mistake when we think pleasure is the way to get happiness. . . . Pleasure is like a dope; gradually we must increase the dose with more excitement, more thrill, more sensation, until, eventually, we find ourselves groping among the tombstones of our dead passions. . . . Our greatest temptation is to put pleasure before God."

—Charles L. Allen, *The Ten Commandments*

Look into it
- David Matzko McCarthy, *The Good Life: Genuine Christianity for the Middle Class*
- Nancy Twigg, *From Clutter to Clarity*
- www.allaboutgod.com/
- www.christianitytoday.com/tcw/9w5/
- www.scrippsnews.com/node/18777

Play the Episode 30 (Lesson 4) clip from the Faith Café DVD. At the conclusion, give the class an opportunity to comment on what they've seen.
- *Did Pastor Gary Burd say anything that challenged you? If so, what was it?*
- *How do we allow our idols to keep us from loving others, particularly the disadvantaged?*
- *How can the idol of materialism blind us to the needs of others? How does it keep us separated from others?*

WALK

Visit people this week who fall into the category often labeled as those "who have so much more." Don't ignore the wealthy because you feel that you don't fit in around them. Remember Jesus' words: "A man's life does not consist in the abundance of his possessions" (Luke 12:15).

The rich, poor, and middle class aren't as different as we feel. We all live under the same commandments, spoken by the one true God. We all feel the lure of temptation toward gods of possessions and thrills.

Go out of your way to get to know someone who has more. Choose to show that person more. Show him or her the love of God living through you.

Take some steps to idol-proof your life during this coming week:

- Survey your material goods. Try to list some ways that you can treat what you own as a blessing from God rather than an idol that keeps you from God.
- Make a log of a particular habit that takes a lot of time, such as TV watching or computer use. Once we recognize the extent of a problem, we can correct it.

This week's spiritual discipline is learning:
This week, choose the discipline of allowing a younger, less experienced person to teach you. Show that you take the other person seriously. Ask questions. Take notes. Realize this can become a deep friendship through which each person learns from the other. Practice humility and love as you sharpen one another.

Before you leave, pass out paper and pens or pencils. Ask the group to write down three ways they can try to minister to someone who has "more" this week. The group can discuss their ideas as time allows. Then have each person write down the name of at least one less experienced person from whom they might try to learn something. Encourage the group to pray about these items and people on their papers throughout the week.

Words: What Am I Saying?

SUPPLIES NEEDED

Names of God on pieces of paper
Paper and pens or pencils

ENTER

"Oh, my God!" "Jesus!" "Thank God!" So what's your guess? Are these quotes from a recent worship service or a football game? Think about it. Why is not taking the Lord's name in vain such a big deal? Does it just mean we shouldn't use curse words? Would this apply to dropping God's name, pretending that we speak for him? In what other situations do you think this command applies? How do we keep this command?

Before class look up some names of God in the Bible and write them on pieces of paper. Alternatively, have your group brainstorm some names of God and write these down. Pass out a name of God to each person. Invite the participants to pray, each person using the name of God that is on their paper either to address God or as a focus for praising God. For instance, someone with the name Comforter on his paper might thank God for providing loving comfort at times of distress.

As we look more closely at this commandment, let's reflect on the idea that everything that comes from our mouths finds its source in our thoughts, minds, and hearts. What do your words say about you?

"For out of the overflow of the heart the mouth speaks."

—Matthew 12:34

Let's think about names. Find someone in the room who:

- was named for a relative.
- often has his or her name misspelled or mispronounced.
- has been a victim of identity theft.
- has repeatedly been called by the wrong name (for example, by a teacher who always referred to him or her with the name of an older sibling).
- has his or her name on a business card or letterhead.
- has ever had his or her name in the newspaper.

Ask each person how that use of his or her name felt.

Consider it

"I have a name; I have to take advantage of it."
—Pierre Cardin, designer

Break the participants into two groups. Have one group discuss positive ways to use a person's name to gain advantage and have the other group discuss negative or deceitful ways to take advantage of a person's name (even their own). After a few minutes, bring the whole group back together and share some of the highlights of your conversations. Ask: Has anyone here ever used his or her name to gain some benefit? Has dropping God's name ever given you an advantage?

DRINK

You shall not misuse the name of the LORD your God, for the LORD will not hold anyone guiltless who misuses his name.

—Exodus 20:7

We often think of this commandment as one limited in scope, only referring to uttering God's name as a curse word. In contrast, the Jews considered this command as one of the most important of the ten.

Rabbis refused to pronounce God's name, (*Yahweh* or *Jehovah*) for fear of misusing it. To this day, many Jews simply call God *HaShem*, meaning "the name" rather than risk using a name for him. Even in writing you may see a Jew type G_d rather than even type the whole word.

Misusing God's name is more than saying it as a curse, but treating his name lightly. How would a king respond if someone pretended to speak for him but instead misrepresented his will? God is likewise displeased by those who use his name for personal gain or to preach hatred. Nor is the name of God a magic incantation that we use to manipulate him by our "holy talk."

We read in the Old Testament that misuse of God's name was a crime worthy of death (Leviticus 24:10-16). Misusing God's name is one way people try to take some of his power and authority and use it as their own—divine identity theft. Who wants to be guilty of that?

═══ GO DEEPER ═══

Each of the commandments is important. All of them came from God as he directed his nation into right paths and corrected them in response to their poor decisions. His people were covered with failures. They had been involved in extreme attacks of what we would label as terrorism. God's chosen nation lived in the middle of a mess.

This command reveals much of God's heart. The warning has deep meaning. The following

words from Dr. Tony Moon, Bible and Ministry professor at Emmanuel College, help us dig deeper into the text.

The third commandment (Exodus 20:7; Deuteronomy 5:11), this prohibition of taking the LORD's name in vain, of "misusing the LORD's name" (NIV), was viewed as one of the most important Old Testament laws in ancient Israel. Rabbis refused even to verbally pronounce the name *Yahweh* for fear of breaking this command. It forbids the abuse of God's name through perjury (lying under oath), witchcraft (in order to manipulate God), and blasphemy (see Leviticus 24:10-16, where "cursing" God is a capital crime).

Stated in a more positive way, this commandment requires that God's name only be uttered in an attitude of respect and reverence. This has direct implications for Christians today. It forbids, of course, the use of God's name in what we commonly call profanity, but it has broader implications as well. For example, do we use the name of God or Jesus (and there are many names and titles for them in the Bible) as an interjection when we are frustrated or angry? Do we have the habit of referring to God or Jesus (or the Holy Spirit) in a context of fun and lightheartedness rather than of worship and prayerfulness?

Ask Dr. Moon's final two questions to the group. Give them time to respond. Again, encourage the class to take notes during the week about what God is saying to them about this study.

●

Besides the NIV verse listed under DRINK, *read some other versions of this commandment. Three are listed below. Then pass out paper and pens or pencils to your group. Have each person reflect on how they would put this commandment into their own words. Have those who are willing share what they write.*

"No using the name of GOD, your God, in curses or silly banter; GOD won't put up with the irreverent use of his name." (The Message)

"You shall not take the name of the LORD your God in vain, for the LORD will not leave him unpunished who takes his name in vain." (NASB)

"Thou shalt not take the name of the LORD thy God in vain; for the LORD will not hold him guiltless that taketh his name in vain." (KJV)

SAVOR

The businessman sat two tables away from me in the restaurant, but it felt as if he were right beside me. It sounded as though his entire life had been wrecked when the waitress brought the wrong order. His words quickly turned her face red: "What's this?!"

She frantically apologized. The man forcefully attacked. He stood up and voiced his bitter disapproval of her mistake. He verbally told her where to go, almost declaring damnation from God toward this young waitress named Rachel.

Suddenly I remembered. "Rachel, I think that was my order," I said. Rachel looked relieved and said to both of us, "I'm so sorry." Another waitress arrived with the other man's meal, just as he ordered it. I smiled. He didn't.

While eating, I could not stop watching the man, still fuming. I prayed for a chance to know more about him. So I walked over. "Is everything OK now?"

He said, "I guess," but I could tell he was lying. Part of me wanted to rebuke him for taking God's name in vain and for treating Rachel so badly. Instead, I asked questions. Carl—he told me his name then—answered with honesty. We talked about his deep pain and broken heart, and I realized the reason for his anger.

The discussion gave me a chance to share my view of God with him. "Carl," I asked, "when you use those words about God and damnation, do you know what that really means and who God really is?" No comment. So I responded by telling him about the God who loves him and the Christ who died for him.

Carl heard my honesty. He thanked me. I could tell he wasn't lying. Before we left the restaurant, he gave me permission to pray for him. I had the honor of talking to Carl about God and then talking to God about Carl. I pray he knows—really knows—the true God, whose name is too holy for us to play games with it.

After reading the story, ask these questions:
- *Have you ever known anyone like Carl? What kind of relationship did you have with this person?*
- *Have you ever had a similar experience of over-hearing someone take God's name in vain in a public place? What did you do?*
- *What do you think you ought to do in this situation?*
- *Have you ever let the way someone talked get in the way of your ministry to them?*

EXPERIENCE

"Religious tolerance is something we should all practice; however, there have been more persecution and atrocities committed in the name of religion and religious freedom than anything else."

—Walter Koenig, actor

Look into it
- Arron Chambers, *Remember Who You Are*
- Ann Spangler, *Praying the Names of Jesus: A Daily Guide*
- http://en.wikipedia.org/wiki/names_of_god_in_Judaism
- www.worldnetdaily.com/news/article.asp?ArtIcLe_ID=51896

WALK

Have you seen the movie *The Ten Commandments*? Schedule a time with your group to watch the film together. Viewing and discussing God's commands can offer a better perspective on both the original meaning and how you can apply it today. Walk the truth this week within community. In addition, meditate on right ways to use God's name.

"And everyone who calls on the name of the Lord will be saved."

—Acts 2:21

Use the name of God to honor him this week:

- Be an ambassador. Ambassadors don't pretend to be the ruler of a country, but recognize that the country will be judged by their actions.
- Be a blessing to someone by doing some kind act in secret: washing their car, shoveling snow off their walk, baking a treat for them. Leave a card that says simply, "Done for you in the name of the Lord."
- Look for other names of God in Scripture and what they say about his character.

This week's spiritual discipline is friendship:

Our discipline this week helps us see others as God sees them. Do you think treating people incorrectly would be a way of taking God's name in vain?

This week, discipline yourself into a spiritual friendship with a nonbeliever. Don't see him as a project, but instead as someone in need of God's grace, just like you.

"Let the name of the Lord be praised,
both now and forevermore.
From the rising of the sun to the place where it sets,
the name of the Lord is to be praised."

—Psalm 113:2, 3

NOTES

Work: Driven from Rest

SUPPLIES NEEDED

White board or chalkboard

Dry-erase marker or chalk

Paper and pens or pencils

Faith Café DVD

ENTER

We are purpose-driven people attending purpose-driven churches and functioning in a variety of purpose-driven roles. And though it's nice to have a purpose, do we have to be so chaotically and stressfully driven?

In our overscheduled world we fail too often to obey God's command: *Remember the Sabbath day.* How many days do you take off from the rush of life? How often do you take time simply to be with God? Not just *doing for* God, but *being with* God?

Begin this week by pausing. Take a deep breath. Close your eyes; relax a few minutes. Picture God with you—you believe he is, don't you?

"It is our best work that God wants, not the dregs of our exhaustion. I think he must prefer quality to quantity."

—George MacDonald

Invite your group to spend a few minutes in silence and rest. Turn off the lights if possible and get rid of as many distractions as you can. After the time of rest, pray: Dear God, thank you for creating this world and for making us able to do your work in it. Help us to remember to take time to rest in you as well. Amen.

Do you know how to relax? Do you get enough rest? Ask yourself:

- How much sleep do I get in a typical night? Enough? Too much?
- What hobbies do I have? Do they help me relax or do they add stress to my life?
- How many nights a month do I have trouble sleeping because of thoughts about work or school?
- Do I feel guilty if I take a break? Do others around me make me feel guilty if I take time to rest?
- Do I ever feel less than mentally sharp during the day because of a lack of rest?
- Are my church activities a help or hindrance to me getting real rest?

Discuss with the group the definition of the term workaholic. *Ask these questions:*

- *How does our culture's obsession with work, performance, success, money, and even leisure affect our willingness to take a Sabbath?*
- *Why do you think God gave us this commandment? What is important about taking a day to rest?*
- *If we don't take time to rest, what might be the result?*

Consider it

"If you rest, you rust."

—Helen Hays, actress

"My soul is more at rest from the tempter when I am busily employed."

—Francis Asbury, English clergyman

Ask the group:
- *Do you agree or disagree with the ideas presented in these two quotes? Why or why not?*
- *Do you think these authors were talking about the same kind of rest as a Sabbath rest? Why or why not?*

Write up on the board the commandment for today. Then underneath that, write Sunday Tasks. Have group members suggest common tasks that they usually have on their list for Sundays. For example: take a jog, do the laundry, cut out coupons, drop kids off at church, iron clothes, cook lunch, choir practice, help kids with homework, etc.

Ask: How many of us put "rest" on our list for Sunday?

DRINK

Remember the Sabbath day by keeping it holy.

—Exodus 20:8

By the seventh day God had finished the work he had been doing; so on the seventh day he rested from all his work. And God blessed the seventh day and made it holy, because on it he rested from all the work of creating that he had done.

—Genesis 2:2, 3

The word *Sabbath* comes from a Hebrew verb, *shabbath,* meaning "to rest." The Sabbath was instituted for mankind. Our creator understands our physical need for rest. The Sabbath gives our minds and bodies time off for rejuvenation and better health. At the heart of the Sabbath is the recognition that we can never work hard enough to meet all of our needs. Yet

God makes up for what we lack when we take time to honor him.

GO DEEPER

The Sabbath is mentioned many other times in the Bible, of course. Read aloud the following two references to the Sabbath in Exodus:

"This is what the LORD commanded: 'Tomorrow is to be a day of rest, a holy Sabbath to the LORD. So bake what you want to bake and boil what you want to boil. Save whatever is left and keep it until morning.'"

—Exodus 16:23

"In six days the LORD made the heavens and the earth, the sea, and all that is in them, but he rested on the seventh day. Therefore the LORD blessed the Sabbath day and made it holy."

—Exodus 20:11

The Sabbath was instituted for mankind. Our creator understands our physical need for rest. The Sabbath gives our minds and bodies time off for rejuvenation and better health.

Encourage each of the participants to read and study each of the following texts. These verses can give a better understanding of the significance of and practice of the Sabbath by Christ and his followers: Matthew 12:1-14; Mark 1:21: 2:23-28: 3:1-5: 16:1, 2; Luke 4:16: 6:1-4: 13:10-17: 14:1-6: 23:56; John 5:1-13: 7:22-24; Acts 13:13-15, 43-45; Hebrews 4:1-11.

SAVOR

Working in a church can be very fulfilling. Working with fellow Christians filled with love, compassion, and spiritual wisdom . . . what could be better than that? So when God opened the door for me to take a secretarial position at my church, I jumped in with both feet!

After a few months, the church administrator offered me the option of changing my work schedule, making Sunday an official workday for me. I quickly accepted the change. I thought this was great; besides, I was *always* at church anyway. Why not make it a workday? It never dawned on me that I would rarely hear a sermon or attend a class.

Many times the commandment to "remember the Sabbath and keep it holy" echoed in my thoughts. I quickly justified my actions, dismissing these gentle whispers of the Holy Spirit. Unfortunately, as time passed, my body became weary, dread began to precede every action, and the longing to escape invaded my thoughts.

You see, I had become so busy doing all the right things *for God* that I found myself out of God's will. Sound crazy? I was neglecting my personal time with the Lord and those I love. Every time the church doors were open I was there. I became angry with myself for my spiritually unhealthy condition and for putting my life in overload.

Convicted by the Holy Spirit, I requested that my work schedule return to its original hours. I reevaluated my responsibilities and turned some things over to others as I realized the full impact of breaking this important commandment. Matthew 11:30 says, "My yoke is easy, and my burden is light." I rediscovered this easy yoke when I chose to obey God's commandment to keep the Sabbath.

(from Loretta J. Eidson,
"The Sabbath Day, Keep It Holy")

Ask the group:
- *What was significant for you about Loretta's story?*
- *Do you see some of yourself in her?*
- *How are the challenges for people in full-time church ministry different from those of church volunteers?*
- *How do you honor the Sabbath if you are required to work on Sunday?*
- *How do we obey this command without becoming legalistic?*

EXPERIENCE

Before I took a one-month sabbatical during my years of pastoring, my friend Garrett Bain wrote this note:

About next month, don't think of it as hiding. This is a time . . . you are going to be completely in God's view. This is his time to expand and develop Chris. Not as a husband, nor as a father or son, not as a coach, friend, pastor, or writer. It's all about Chris. It's a sabbatical, rest and recharging. Stepping outside of what you normally do so you have a fresh perspective when you step back into it.

Look into it
- Marva Dawn, *Keeping the Sabbath Wholly*
- Eugene Peterson, *Christ Plays in Ten Thousand Places*
- http://www.willowcreek.org/news/sabbath/default.asp
- http://www.gracethrufaith.com/ask-a-bible-teacher/our-sabbath-rest

Play the Episode 32 (Lesson 6) clip from the Faith Café DVD, which features an interview with singer/songwriter Margaret Becker. Invite the group to share their comments in response to these questions:
- *Did any of Margaret Becker's actions to create peace and simplicity inspire you to slow your life pace?*
- *If so, what is a first step you can take toward relieving the stress in your life?*
- *Who or what suffers in your life because of unwillingness to slow down?*
- *What do you value most? How does your life reflect those values?*

WALK

Create an order of worship for your Sabbath experience. First, list times you find true rest at church, at home, or out with friends. Write the words of a hymn or other song that help you relax and focus on God. Draw or write about what reminds you of rest. Through your week, take your Sabbath list with you. Let it remind you of your need to rest in assurance that God cares for you and meets your needs.

You might consider ending this week's session in a similar way to the beginning. Take some time to rest together and then close with a simple prayer, asking for God to give his peace to each participant.

Have a Sabbath open house:

- Don't make it a lot of work! Have a simple meal of pizza and salad or make it a potluck.
- Make a point to invite people you know who are "weary and burdened."
- Take a leisurely walk together in a nearby park or around your neighborhood. At home, light candles, play soft music, and just relax together.
- If needed, provide quiet activities for children in a separate area (drawing, modeling clay, books, a DVD, etc.)
- Close the time with a simple prayer or reading a Bible verse that talks about rest.

This week's spiritual discipline is humility:

Humility, or decreasing ourselves, reminds us what matters most. Like Sabbath rest, humility helps us gain a healthier view of life, God, and ourselves. We recognize that we do not have to make everything happen, that just as God has instituted life principles for us, he will be faithful to take care of us.

"I feel as if God had, by giving the Sabbath, given fifty-two springs in every year."
—*Samuel Taylor Coleridge*

NOTES

Family: Do We Honor God?

SUPPLIES NEEDED

White board or chalkboard

Dry-erase markers or chalk

Faith Café DVD

Small live tree or big picture of a tree

Paper and pens or pencils

Handout that includes the image of a tree and room for member to draw or write

ENTER

From the very beginning of time, families have been dysfunctional. Biblical parents failed their children in any number of ways. The first family was marked by fratricide (Genesis 4:8). Jacob's favoritism caused Joseph to be a target among his brothers. David's impotent anger at sexual abuse within his family would tear the whole country apart. But despite parental failings, the family still can provide blessings no other institution can.

Before engaging in conversation with others today, ask God to help you understand the point of this study and hear what he has to say to you. Perhaps you have a relationship with your parents that needs healing. Or maybe you are a parent struggling to connect with your kids. Ask God for guidance, believing he can and will answer your request.

Note for the leader: Your group will likely experience a variety of feelings when discussing family history. Consider the mix of backgrounds that may exist in your group: adopted children, children of single parent families, those who had babies out of wedlock, those raised by people other than their biological parents, those whose parents are no longer with them, those who suffered abuse or neglect, those who grew up in believing homes and those who did not. Be sensitive to the vast array of circumstances. Before diving into the study, you may want to pray for the group, confessing the variety of thoughts and feeling that might emerge and asking God to touch each person in his or her own situation.

Spend a few moments considering your relationship with your parents.

- How often do you talk to your mother or father?
- How has your relationship with them developed over the past few years?
- What phrases your parents said to you when you were young do you still remember?
- How do you want to be like your parents?
- How do you hope to be different?

What reminders of your past have these questions unearthed in you?

Consider it

"Perhaps the greatest social service that can be rendered by anybody to the country and to mankind is to bring up a family."

—George Bernard Shaw

Discuss the Consider it *quote with your group.*
- *In what ways might this statement be true?*
- *What do you think George Bernard Shaw meant exactly by "bring up" a family?*
- *How important do you think family life is in the culture of a country?*
- *In what ways did your parents succeed at providing a social service for you and your siblings?*

DRINK

Honor your father and your mother, so that you may live long in the land the LORD your God is giving you.
—Exodus 20:12

This week's commandment provides something the previous commands did not . . . a promise. Attached to the rule is a pledge from God that matched the deep desire of the Israelites and matches the desire of us all.

The promise? Obey this command, and the days the Lord God gives you in the land shall be many. While this doesn't guarantee a certain number of years of life, and it doesn't assure the obedient ones that they can live in the Promised Land for a particular length of time, it does reveal the result of obedience. God blesses those who obey him.

GO DEEPER

What did God mean by this word *honor*? How can and should people honor their parents? Is this a commandment just for young children, or does it apply regardless of one's age? Does it apply to those whose parents mistreat them?

These are good questions. The Bible is filled with Scriptures that make this applicable to all situations. These Scriptures also make clear the way parents are instructed to treat their children and the principle that obedience to God is the highest priority.

Ask group members to read the following Scriptures. Remind them of the importance of understanding each command in its context.

These texts can help complete our understanding of this week's command: Deuteronomy 6:6, 7; Proverbs 22:6; Mark 7:9-13; Luke 2:51; Ephesians 6:1-4; Colossians 3:20, 21; 1 Timothy 5:4.

God's command to honor parents can mean many things. Here are some suggestions for ways to live it out:

- Speak well of parents to others.
- Speak well to parents. Be polite to them.
- Show respect and courtesy to parents.
- Forgive any wrong parents have done, remembering they are also born in sin and in need of redemption, forgiveness, and healing.
- Consider seeing a Christian counselor when family pain controls or influences other relationships too deeply.
- Pray for your parents.
- Go through family photo albums: rejoice about the good, release the hurt, and forgive those who wronged you.

SAVOR

Gary sat on the other side of the wall. I was free. I could move around and leave when I wanted. But Gary?

We talked. Gary told me again of his poor treatment, of his legitimate reason for the actions that had landed him here, of how much longer he would remain in solitary confinement, and of how much longer he would be in prison.

As Gary moved from defending himself to a discussion of his own mistakes, he responded to my questions. I asked, "What really put you here? Drugs? Friends? The women? What took you from how you were as a child, when I watched you play ball, to the place you are now?"

Gary paused as he sat on the prison cell floor in silence. "I treated Mom and Dad so bad. Always mean. Talking with a smart mouth. I was hateful to them. I saw my friends having fun. My parents said no whenever I asked to do something they labeled inappropriate. They always made me go to church. I hated boring church. It seemed so stupid and pointless to me. But I had to go anyway."

"What else, Gary?"

"You know. I wanted to date this girl, but my parents insisted she wasn't the right one for me. That was all I could take. I decided to start doing everything they told me not to do."

Gary kicked the floor. He kicked it again as he yelled with volume. These emotional outbursts continued even after much counseling and many sessions of anger management. However, he stopped sooner this time. He came right toward our little window and said, "I'm sorry. You know how I am."

"Tell me, Gary," I said. "Tell me how you really are."

He lifted his shoulders, shrugging off my question. But I saw his eyes. Gary knew something. Then in a way I didn't expect, Gary started describing two people. One was the man Gary had become. He talked about sex, drugs, anger, and prison life. He also described another young man. "The man I should have been," Gary called him.

"I could have been him," Gary said. "Why didn't I listen to my parents? That could have saved so much pain. For them. For me. Why didn't I listen to them?"

We talked longer. We prayed. We worked out a time to meet again. As I walked away, I thought about how many people need to hear Gary's honesty.

After reading Gary's story, ask the group these questions:
- *What about Gary's story speaks to you?*
- *How much do you think family relationships play a part in the crime rate we have today?*
- *What are some things you could do to encourage someone who is having a hard time getting along with their parents?*

EXPERIENCE

A survey by the International Union of Gospel Missions indicated that troubled families perpetuate themselves. The majority of homeless heads of families (mostly women) were not raised in intact homes (51%). In all, 18% spent time in foster homes, and 30% never had a father at home.

Look into it
- Ken Davis, *How to Live With Your Parents Without Losing Your Mind*
- www.crosswalk.com/family/parenting/1424445.html
- www.topical-bible-studies.org/18-0005.htm

Play the Episode 33 (Lesson 7) clip from the Faith Café DVD, featuring comedians Bean and Bailey. After watching the video, have the group members use the humorous song and the following questions to jumpstart discussion:
- *As adults, what are some ways that we honor our parents?*
- *Bean and Bailey humorously sing about the common modern phenomenon of grown children coming back to live at home with parents. Although there is often no moral problem with this situation, what other things does our culture find acceptable that, as Christians, we should evaluate as we seek to obey this week's command?*
- *How does respect factor into this commandment?*

WALK

Place the tree or picture of a tree in a location where everyone can see it. This prop can be used to inspire group members in the following activity. Pass out paper and pens or pencils.

Sketch out your own family tree. Go back as far in your family history as you can. What relatives influenced you most? How are you different today than you would have been without their influence? What would be an appropriate way to honor them?

If the relationship with your own parents is a broken one, think and pray this week about how it might be restored. You might start by writing a letter of thanks to your mom or dad. Try to focus on the positive side of your relationship.

If your parents are either not living or not around, think about older people in your community who need to be treated with respect. Remember to honor your heavenly Father by keeping his command to love one another.

Remind the participants to think about these questions throughout the week. Leave them with this thought: God does not gossip about, condemn, or give up on us. He is a faithful and loving Father, who is able to guide us safely toward the changes we need to make.

This week, make it a priority to do these two things:

- Pray for family members.
- Connect with family members (in person, by phone, or e-mail). Let love, forgiveness, and kindness flavor every word you use.
- If making these connections is tough for you, enlist the help of a friend, pastor, or counselor. Don't give up. Let God transform you and your relationships.

This week's spiritual discipline is assessment:

Most of us do not rejoice when it's test time. Evaluations frighten us. Remember your last trip to the doctor for a checkup?

But life is too important and spiritual growth is too vital to go unexamined. This week, apply the spiritual discipline of assessment. Be honest with yourself to see how you're really doing in your spiritual journey. Is your relationship with God a living one?

NOTES

Encourage participants to apply the spiritual discipline of assessment. Avoid sounding judgmental or condemning. Instead, help group members see this exercise as a means of protection and improvement. In order to help everyone prepare, ask questions like these:

- *How am I applying what we're learning each week?*
- *Do those around me notice any difference in my life?*
- *In what ways have I felt God calling me to change?*
- *What areas of my life do I need to let God use to transform me?*

Hatred: Murder in Our Hearts

SUPPLIES NEEDED

Newspapers
White board or chalkboard
Dry-erase markers or chalk
Faith Café DVD

ENTER

Allow these words and phrases to bring mental images to mind: *9/11, World Trade Center, ethnic cleansing, suicide bombers, Iraq, Iran, nuclear weapons, plane crash, terrorism, gang violence, police brutality.*

No doubt some of the images that came to your mind were televised on the news. What caused these images to be? What attitudes about the value of life may be found at the root of these situations?

How can we change a world that treats life as disposable, that makes human beings a target of people's anger, and that pits one nation or ethnic group against another?

"By this may all know that we are not his disciples, because we hate one another."
—Robert Leighton, Scottish preacher

Pass out portions of newspapers. You may need to have several newspapers depending on the size of your group. Let each of the participants have time to look through the papers and search for stories that involve violent conflict or deaths. Ask the following questions to start discussion:

- *How many of you watch the news or read news stories regularly? How do you feel when you read about stories like the ones found in these papers?*
- *Does it bother you to read about this type of violence in your world?*
- *Does it make a difference to you whether the violence is happening on your street, or in your city, or in your state, or in your world?*
- *How would you feel if you were a family member of one of those victims in these stories? (Remember to be sensitive to the fact that some in your group may actually be or know someone who was a victim of violence.)*
- *How do you think some of these conflicts began? What attitudes, beliefs, or thoughts do you think contributed to the escalation of violence?*
- *Do you think the violence was justified in any of the stories you found? If so, why?*

How about you? How do your attitudes reflect the value you place on human life? Ask yourself:

- How do I act toward a driver that cuts me off in traffic?
- How have I allowed violent movies and television programs to desensitize me to the harsh realities of war, crime, and violence?
- What assumptions do I make about people simply because of the way they look, dress, or speak?
- How often have I taken my anger out on someone, not because he or she was guilty, but because he or she was handy?

Have the group discuss this quote:
- *What do people think G. K. Chesterton was talking about?*
- *Do they agree with him?*
- *What obstacles make it so difficult to love our enemies?*

DRINK

You shall not murder.

—Exodus 20:13

You have heard that it was said to the people long ago, "Do not murder, and anyone who murders will be subject to judgment." But I tell you that anyone who is angry with his brother will be subject to judgment. Again, anyone who says to his brother, "Raca," is answerable to the Sanhedrin. But anyone who says, "You fool!" will be in danger of the fire of hell.

—Matthew 5:21, 22

The word translated *kill* or *murder* in this week's text is not the only Hebrew word used in the Old Testament with reference to killing. This word emphasizes a deliberate, calculated taking of human life. Even before the time of Moses, God clearly differentiated between murder and taking the life of an animal. Humans were allowed to kill animals for food, but established civil authorities were to punish homicide by execution (Genesis 9:1-6). This distinction continued in Mosaic law (Exodus 21:12-36).

Centuries later, Jesus expanded the reach of the sixth commandment, interpreting it in a way that surprised even the most religious of his day. Jesus stated that we cannot just refrain from murder, but must also monitor our emotions, our motives, and our hearts.

GO DEEPER

Read the Beatitudes from Matthew 5:1-12.

Now when he saw the crowds, he went up on a mountainside and sat down. His disciples came to him, and he began to teach them, saying:

"Blessed are the poor in spirit,
for theirs is the kingdom of heaven.
Blessed are those who mourn,
for they will be comforted.
Blessed are the meek,
for they will inherit the earth.
Blessed are those who hunger and
thirst for righteousness,
for they will be filled.
Blessed are the merciful,
for they will be shown mercy.
Blessed are the pure in heart,
for they will see God.
Blessed are the peacemakers,
for they will be called sons of God.
Blessed are those who are persecuted
because of righteousness,
for theirs is the kingdom of heaven.

Blessed are you when people insult you, persecute you and falsely say all kinds of evil against you because of me. Rejoice and be glad, because great is your reward in heaven, for in the same way they persecuted the prophets who were before you."

The first four commandments highlight our relationship with God. The next six offer guidelines for living in community. We aren't alone, and we should not live as if we were. People are all around us, and God gives us instructions on how to live this life with others. This sixth commandment instructs us to value life. After reading the Beatitudes, discuss with your group how the thinking presented in those verses might help us understand and live out not only the command not to murder, but all of the Ten Commandments.

SAVOR

He was a remarkable man with an all-too-typical story. Born in the Middle East, his environment was filled with violence. His religion was divided into competing sects, two of which were the most powerful and always at odds with one another. The fundamentalist sect included a majority of his countrymen, but the more secular wing held the political power in the immediate region.

A quick mind allowed him to study hard and grasp the intricate arguments and traditions associated with the fundamentalist group. But religious zeal seemed to fuel his violent nature rather than tame it.

As a rising star among adherents of his religion, he used his prominence to wield power. He united with his religious foes against a common enemy—a small but growing fringe element of their religion. Fundamentalist zeal merged with political authority and became a deadly combination. With devout fervor, he rounded up members of the new religion, leading to the capture and death of many.

In the midst of this campaign, the extraordinary occurred. The persecutor joined the persecuted. Rabbi Saul of Tarsus rejected the fundamentalism of the sect of the Pharisees, flaunted the political influence of the Sadducees, and became a Christian!

Faith in Jesus did more than give him another cause. It gave him another life. Years later he would write, "I was once a blasphemer and a persecutor and a violent man, [but] I was shown mercy." Murderous rage was replaced by grace in the life of the man we now know as the apostle Paul.

Ask the group these questions:
- *If you'd read the story of Saul the persecutor changing his ways and turning to Christ in today's paper, what would you have thought? Would you have doubted the story's truth or perhaps the man's sincerity?*
- *What do you think when you hear of a convict who becomes born again in prison? Does how you feel depend on how bad their crime was? Why or why not?*

- *God showed mercy to Saul, as he does to all of us. But are there times when we think it's almost OK not to forgive or show mercy? What are those times?*
- *What can we do to get closer to seeing people the way God sees them?*

EXPERIENCE

"Power is when we have every justification to kill, and we don't."
—said by Oskar Schindler, in *Schindler's List*

"We can kill by killing with thoughts or ideals. In talking about a man who had leaped from the window of a high building, an [elderly acquaintance] very wisely said, 'When a man has lost God, there ain't nothing he can do but jump.'"
—Charles L. Allen, *The Ten Commandments*

Play the Episode 34 (Lesson 8) clip from the Faith Café DVD. At the conclusion of the segment, discuss Lily Isaacs's interview. Use the following conversation starters:
- *Is hate ever justified? Explain your response.*
- *How are we to deal with people who cause us extreme pain?*
- *What are some examples, other than the Holocaust, when Christians have justified their hatred and violence? Is this OK? Why or why not?*
- *What does Jesus teach us about this topic?*

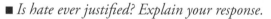

Look into it
- Oswald Chambers, *Studies in the Sermon on the Mount*
- *Glory*, Sony Pictures, 1998
- *Saving Private Ryan*, DreamWorks Video, 1999
- *Schindler's List*, Universal Studios, 2004
- *World Trade Center*, Paramount, 2006
- www.sojo.net/
- www.tektonics.org/lp/nokilling.htm

WALK

Has God been speaking to you recently about your need to forgive a particular person or group? If so, pray what Jesus prayed during his Sermon on the Mount—the Lord's Prayer. Meditate on these lines: "Forgive us our debts, as we also have forgiven our debtors" (Matthew 6:12). Remember that God does not always immediately remove our struggles. You may have to make a daily choice to cooperate with God and forgive those who have hurt you. That is OK.

Nor does forgiveness automatically restore a relationship. By forgiving you forfeit your right to take vengeance into your own hands. But forgiveness is *not* giving permission for someone to hurt you again. Allow God to dictate the timetable for restoration.

Consider taking this message one step further:

- Get permission from a local corrections facility to write a letter, offering hope for forgiveness in Christ, to a convicted murderer.
- Contact a local prison ministry and find out how you can be involved with their outreach to inmates in your community.

This week's spiritual discipline is harmony:

Blending differences, learning from one another, and allowing our individual distinctions to make us stronger are much better and more Christlike actions than criticizing, hating, or seeking to harm others, even if only with our words. Rather than looking down on people who are unlike us, we can gain a better grasp of God's will as we harmonize.

NOTES

Fantasy: Just One Look

SUPPLIES NEEDED

Optional DVD clips or ads

White board or chalkboard

Dry-erase markers or chalk

Faith Café DVD

ENTER

Think of the computer screen . . . the television . . . the magazine behind the counter. It's just one peek, one glance. What does it matter, anyway? It doesn't hurt anyone . . . or does it?

Sexual sin is seen as no big deal in our culture. It is a private matter, people say. But our experiences tell us a different story. Looks have become longings. "Innocent" desires have changed our thoughts. Unchecked urges have led us into places where we have sworn we would never go.

As news reports continue relating stories about the latest mistakes of our leaders, how are we affected? Do we ever think it could happen to us? Whether we are married or not, how do the movies, TV shows, books, Internet sites, or images we immerse ourselves in shape our attitudes about adultery? And what do we do about that?

Allow time for the group members to discuss their views about adultery in the media. You might want to talk about how it's often treated as a laughing matter or how romantic films sometimes lead the audience to root for the adulterous couple to get together. You could bring clips of DVDs to illustrate your point, or examples of sexually charged advertising (just make sure the material is appropriate for the discussion). Here are some other questions to explore:

- *Do you think the amount of sexuality depicted in mainstream television shows and advertising is the same as when you were a kid? What effect, if any, do you think sexuality in advertising has on children today?*
- *What do you think plays a greater role in the development of people's attitudes about sex and adultery—how sex and marriage is depicted in the media or how it is handled at home?*

Let's take a look at how we are tempted with lust from day to day:

- Think of a few TV or print advertisements that are currently popular. How do these ads appeal to lust to sell products?
- Consider a popular TV program or movie. How is human sexuality dealt with in it? How does that compare to Bible teaching? How does it compare to your personal experience? Does it tell the whole story about sex and lust or avoid dealing with certain consequences? If it were accurate in its depictions, how would the plot be different?

Consider it

"Love begins with an image; lust with a sensation."
—Mason Cooley, writer

Does the group agree or disagree with this comment? Why or why not? Is lust only a physical feeling, or are there emotional, mental, and spiritual elements to it as well?

DRINK

You shall not commit adultery.

—Exodus 20:14

Flee from sexual immorality. All other sins a man commits are outside his body, but he who sins sexually sins against his own body. Do you not know that your body is a temple of the Holy Spirit, who is in you, whom you have received from God? You are not your own; you were bought at a price. Therefore honor God with your body.

—1 Corinthians 6:18-20

GO DEEPER

Don't avoid discussing this topic out of a fear that it is irrelevant or will be uninteresting for those who aren't married. Everyone needs to be reminded of what God considers to be healthy sexual behavior and what our duties and obligations to one another are.

This week's Scripture is brief. The command is short, but history proves it is not easily obeyed.

Read Genesis 2:18-24 to the class:

The LORD God said, "It is not good for the man to be alone. I will make a helper suitable for him."

Now the LORD God had formed out of the ground all the beasts of the field and all the birds of the air. He brought them to the man to see what he would name them; and whatever the man called each living creature, that was its name. So the man gave names to all the livestock, the birds of the air and all the beasts of the field.

But for Adam no suitable helper was found. So the LORD God caused the man to fall into a deep sleep; and while he was sleeping, he took one of the man's ribs and closed up the place with flesh. Then the LORD God made a woman from the rib he had taken out of the man, and he brought her to the man.

The man said,
"This is now bone of my bones,
and flesh of my flesh;
she shall be called 'woman,'
for she was taken out of man."

For this reason a man will leave his father and mother and be united to his wife, and they will become one flesh.

Ask these questions:
- Why did God place Adam and Eve together?
- What do you think is significant about the following words and phrases from the Genesis passage: *leave, united, become one flesh?*
- Though we often highlight the sexual aspects of "becoming one flesh," what else might God have in mind? (Guide the conversation to ideas such as love, acceptance, forgiveness, listening, caring, giving, dying to self, respect, and honor.)

God included the commandment about adultery in a world where men married many women and could have physical relationships with concubines. But was that what God wanted? Look at Proverbs 6:27-29:

Can a man scoop fire into his lap
without his clothes being burned?
Can a man walk on hot coals
without his feet being scorched?
So is he who sleeps with another
man's wife;
no one who touches her will go
unpunished.

The answer, of course, is that God wants the godly person's life to follow his original design. Lustful desires should not be allowed to guide us in our decision-making processes. But how do we defeat these natural tendencies in a world surrounding us with lust-producing temptations?

The following is Paul's response to this difficult situation (1 Corinthians 6:18–7:5):

Flee from sexual immorality. All other sins a man commits are outside his body, but he who sins sexually sins against his own body. Do you not know that your body is a temple of the Holy Spirit, who is in you, whom you have received from God? You are not your own; you were bought at a price. Therefore honor God with your body.

Now for the matters you wrote about: It is good for a man not to marry. But since there is so much immorality, each man should have his own wife, and each woman her own husband. The husband should fulfill his marital duty to his wife, and likewise the wife to her husband. The wife's body does not belong to her alone but also to her husband. In the same way, the husband's body does not belong to him alone but also to his wife. Do not deprive each other except by mutual consent and for a time, so that you may devote yourselves to prayer. Then come together again so that Satan will not tempt you because of your lack of self-control.

The body—the temple of God's Spirit—must remain clean and must function according to God's design in order for God to live inside us. God voiced the seventh commandment to Moses because he knew that sexual sin, more powerful and insidious than any military foes, could defeat his people. It can also defeat us today, if we do not guard against it.

SAVOR

Do you crave and lust for more than God allows? Remember this: Jesus can help. And maybe . . . sex is not what our souls and hearts are looking for. Jesus fulfills our deepest desire for love and acceptance. Here is a story that shows us how he does . . .

I wonder how Zacchaeus felt when he first learned of Christ's arrival. We do not know how long Zacchaeus knew of the event prior to its occurrence. His eagerness to see Jesus, however, reveals some level of intense anticipation.

For Zacchaeus, life as usual consisted of a nice income linked to a terrible social life. As the chief tax collector, people enjoyed seeing him show up about as much as a famine. . . . Crookedness was as much a part of the vocation as the needed knowledge of accounting.

When this "sawed off little social disaster" heard Jesus was going to be traveling in his direction, he reacted with zeal. He did not have friends or a good reputation, but he knew one thing. Zacchaeus wanted to see the man he regularly heard about. He wanted to see who Jesus was or what he was or what he could do for him. . . .

Peter had to venture out of a boat onto tumultuous water. Bartimaeus had to cry loudly to be heard above the commotion. Zacchaeus wanted to see Jesus. If he wanted it badly enough, he had to do something about it.

Most of us dream. In our imaginations we write songs, we devise new inventions, we enjoy popularity, we amass great wealth. Dreams do not materialize without effort. The majority of people never advance past the dream stage. Many run out of steam before the finish line.

In our spiritual lives we are faced with a choice. We can hope of drawing near to Jesus, but the fulfillment of that hunger will lie dormant until we take action. Zacchaeus's desire to see Jesus began to move toward fulfillment when he took action.

The decisions of Zacchaeus have provided fuel for countless songs and sermons over the years. A short guy climbing a tree to see over the heads of a crowd intrigues us. Discouragement over his stature and the size of an audience could have derailed the pursuit of his dream. Zacchaeus did not let that stop him; his determination overruled his dilemma. He implemented his plan of seeing Jesus by climbing the now famous sycamore tree.

(adapted from Chris Maxwell,
Beggars Can Be Chosen)

Ask the group these questions:
- *What do you and Zacchaeus have in common?*
- *What can you learn from his lesson?*
- *What is in the way of your being the person God is calling you to be?*
- *How can we help one another become people who are eagerly seeking more of Jesus in our lives?*

EXPERIENCE

"From the verse, 'The . . . adulterer waits for twilight saying, No eye shall see me' (Job 24:15), the Talmud identifies the adulterer as a practical atheist, since he does not say, no *man* shall see me, but no *eye*—neither the eye of one below nor the eye of him above."

—www.levitt.com/hebrew/commandments.html

Play the Episode 35 (Lesson 9) clip from the Faith Café DVD and listen as Jason Illian, former contestant on the popular television show The Bachelorette, *talks from his experience. Ask these questions:*
- *How would you define promiscuity?*
- *How would you define adultery?*
- *Did anything that was said in this interview resonate with you? If so, what?*
- *How can single people like Jason apply the commandment not to commit adultery?*
- *What could people who are not now married do to guard against adulterous behavior in any future relationships?*
- *How can single people support married friends in their attempt to keep this commandment?*
- *What does your church do to help people stay faithful in their marriages? What does your church do when people engage in adultery?*

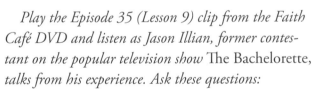

Look into it
- Nancy C. Anderson, *Avoiding the Greener Grass Syndrome*
- Jason B. Illian, *Undressed*
- Kevin Leman, *Sheet Music*
- Gary Smalley and John Trent, *Love Is a Decision*
- Lauren Winner, *Real Sex*
- www.christianitytoday.com/marriage

WALK

"If one wants another only for some self-satisfaction, usually in the form of sensual pleasure, that wrong desire takes the form of lust rather than love."

—Mortimer Adler, philosopher

Committing adultery is an act of selfish disobedience. Love is giving and allowing ourselves to be of service to another. Lust is taking and making someone else be of service to us. Make a commitment to do what is, in a sense, the opposite of committing adultery—by giving instead of taking.

Consider taking these actions this week:

- Instead of satisfying that desire or craving for something or someone you know you shouldn't have, choose to give. Find an item that you own and love, and give it away.
- Rediscover what God wants us to know about love. Meditate on 1 Corinthians 13.

This week's spiritual discipline is reflection:
The discipline of reflection requires discernment. We need to evaluate ourselves using God's truth as our guide. Why should we reflect? Periodically we all need to know how we're really doing and whether we are moving forward in this faith journey. After realizing how you are growing, changing, and developing, you can then determine what hinders or helps you. Are you holding onto hurt? repeatedly falling into the same sin? forgiving? growing? Set aside some time to reflect on where you are spiritually.

LOOK FURTHER

Polls show us that the divorce rate among Christians is about the same as that among non-Christians. Indeed, this comparison has been true for quite some time. You may want to discuss with your group their reactions to this fact. Is it surprising? Why or why not?

Think about what the state of the divorce rate says about Christianity. Some people may think it doesn't matter much—everyone experiences marital troubles, everyone makes mistakes, why should Christians be any different?

But outsiders looking in on the Christian faith may find the divorce rate very significant indeed. Look at these comments from the Web site godisimaginary.com:

So let's review. When a Christian couple gets married, we have all of these forces that should be working to keep them married:

1. The marriage is performed in God's presence . . .

2. in God's house . . .

3. in front of God's representative (a minister or priest) . . .

4. and in front of many Christian witnesses.

5. The couple presumably prays before and after the wedding for a good marriage . . .

6. as do all of the witnesses . . .

7. and the minister/priest.

8. The couple knows that if they divorce/remarry, it is an act of adultery . . .

9. which God has forbidden . . .

10. and which the Bible says is punishable by death.

And don't forget this important line from the ceremony: **What God has joined together let no man put asunder.** Now think about this. God is the all-powerful, all-knowing creator of the universe. If God puts something together, shouldn't it be impossible to break it? Isn't that what "all-powerful" means?

The writer of this material, an atheist, uses the fact of the divorce rate among Christians as his proof number 38 of why God is imaginary. The writer goes on to say:

Given all of this, and given the fact that an all-powerful, prayer-answering God is supposedly looking over the lives of a Christian couple, guiding them in the spirit and so on, what would you expect the divorce rate for Christians to be? Clearly, the Christian divorce rate should be *zero*. . . .

The reason for the high divorce rate among Christians is easy to see: God is imaginary.

Now granted, the writer's logic has some holes in it, but the point is well taken. Just consider all the stories you have heard in the last decade of adultery and sexual immorality ruining the marriages and careers of well-known Christian leaders. Shouldn't all areas of the lives of Christians reflect their faith in Jesus? If we can't keep our marriages intact, and marriage is a metaphor for Christ's relationship with the church, what might that say about how serious Christians are about their faith?

NOTES

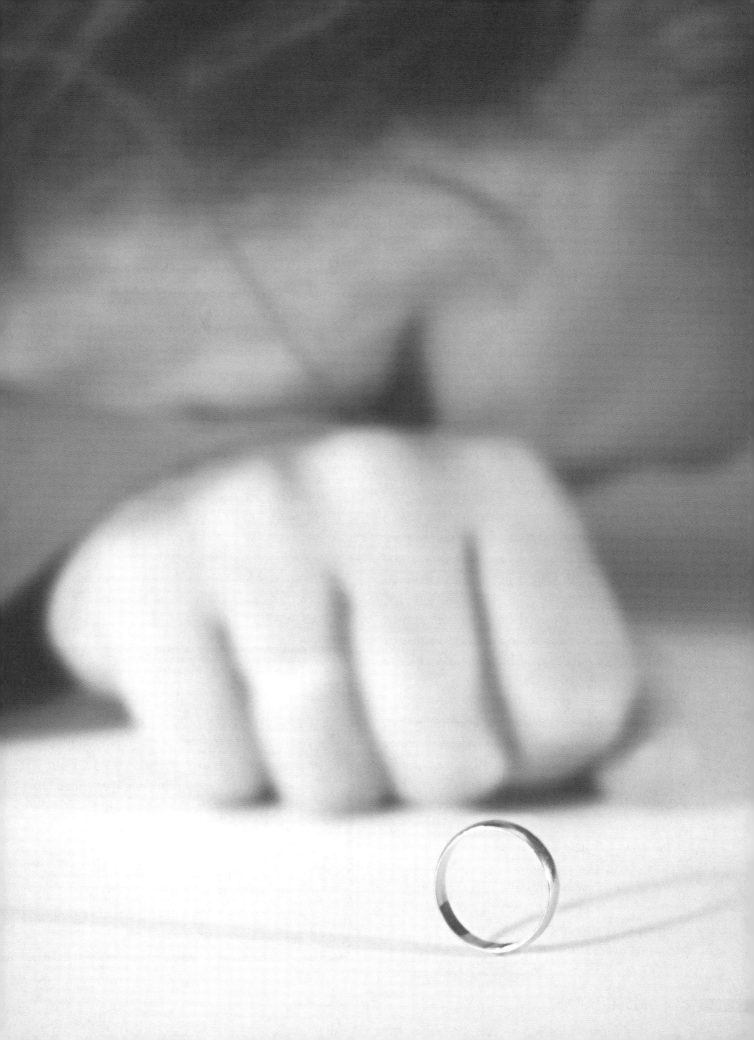

Theft: Who Are We Cheating?

SUPPLIES NEEDED

Faith Café DVD

White board or chalkboard

Dry-erase markers or chalk

ENTER

Four words. *Thou shalt not steal.* No discussion. No argument. God commands. Man obeys. Is it that easy?

Well, we want it to be. But it often isn't. That is why we need to understand the truth. That is also why we need to seek better ways of living truly. Notice the word here—*we*. Faith Café is not about individuals making singular attempts at obeying what God says. It is all of us here . . . together . . . in community. Each time we gather we should ask God to infuse us with an ability to understand his truth and with the humility to live it out.

There is no better place to learn, talk, grow, struggle, laugh, cry, share, celebrate, and grieve than with our fellow Christians, our fellow travelers. Together with God and one another, honestly dialogue this surprisingly complex commandment as you seek to discover what it means for today's believer.

Allow some time to discuss this quote. It's a humorous one, and we can talk about the funny aspects of life in the suburbs and how everything starts to look the same. But there's a serious side to this idea of identity theft as well. Here are some questions to consider:

- *Have you ever felt the need to suppress a part of yourself in order to blend in with the people around you? Did you ever think of this as a way of cheating others out of knowing you?*
- *If everyone in Faith Café were to get up and go visit your house right now, would you be OK with that? Why or why not? Are there things in your house you feel you'd need to hide? (People may answer this to themselves.)*
- *Do you ever buy things on credit because you feel you need to have them to keep up with the times, but you don't want to wait until you have the money? What motivates these purchases? Did you ever think of this as a way you steal from yourself?*
- *Do you ever wish you could steal someone else's identity for a day? Who would you want to be, and why?*

How sticky are your fingers? Ask yourself:

- How many pens do you have in your pocket or purse? Did you buy them, or did you take them from your workplace?
- Look at the material you are now reading—is it an original or a photocopy? How many times have you photocopied something rather than bought it?
- Do you treat electronic property the same as "hard" property? Do you have illegal copies of songs, movies, or software?
- Is every line on your tax return or expense report always accurate?

DRINK

You shall not steal.

—Exodus 20:15

Did you used to make ends meet by stealing? Well, no more! Get an honest job so that you can help others who can't work.

—Ephesians 4:28 *(The Message)*

The eighth commandment summarizes a detailed series of laws of the Jews concerning property rights (Exodus 22:1-15). While we are warned not to worship our material goods, the Bible clearly defends even the weakest person's right to have what is his.

GO DEEPER

We have made our way to the eighth commandment. This command instructs God's people to refrain from robbing, stealing, or taking from others what doesn't belong to them.

Readers and hearers of the original text knew this meant taking from people or nations without permission. In our day, how does this commandment apply? How far should we take it? Think in terms of spending money that isn't yours, or removing others' possessions without their knowledge, or withholding payments you have agreed to make. That makes it a little more relevant, doesn't it?

God wanted his people to be givers rather than takers. God wanted them to be truthful in their words and actions. God wanted them to live beyond the normal lifestyle of pleasing self. God wanted them to be different and loving. God

wanted them to obey his commands. God wants that for us.

Use the following teaching from Rabbi Barry H. Block to confront the ongoing struggles we all face as we learn from this text. His words give us insight into the Jewish understanding of this commandment. They also challenge us to choose God's way even when no one is watching. (Faith Café thanks Rabbi Block for his permission to use his teaching. Encourage participants to visit this link to read his entire sermon at www.beth-elsa.org/bb021706.htm.)

Thou Shalt Not Steal:
A Controversial Commandment?

Let us consider the music-lover, who downloads songs onto her iPod without paying for the right to do so. And what about the small business that buys a couple of licenses for a program that several of its employees must use and then copies the software onto multiple computers?

[As tax season arrives, how] many restaurant workers will declare, as part of their income, less than the full amount they received in tips? How many wealthy people will fail to declare complicated sources of income that are hard to trace? How many others will find myriads of methods of cheating on their taxes, in ways that are most unlikely to be detected? And how many of us will think of them as thieves? Aren't taxes basically bad anyway? Wouldn't a person be silly to pay taxes that he or she could get away without paying? And how many have argued that the tax valuation of their home was too high, only to seek quite a bit more when the time comes to sell?

All too often, as we seek to get the best financial deal for ourselves, we rationalize that "everyone does it." We imagine that our crime has no victim, and is, therefore, no crime at all. Who among us wants to be the sucker, paying what the law would truly require, when we presume that few others do so?

Who is the victim? The multimillionaire rock star? The distant and incredibly successful software company? The evil Internal Revenue Service and the faceless government?

This week's Torah portion suggests that the victim is none other than God. Yes, we may divide the Ten Commandments among those that regulate relations between human beings, and others that speak specifically to our interactions with God. Certainly, "Thou shalt not steal" is among the mitzvot [commandments] that involve our treatment of others. Nevertheless, God is the M'tzaveh, the Commander. When we transgress these laws, we harm the divine image. We alienate ourselves from God.

When we steal, in whatever form, we place our own temporal needs above what is right. If our highest standard is, "I won't get caught," we have joined ourselves to the lowest level of humanity. We are no different from the stick-up man. We are thieves. We are part of the crowd that engages in wrongdoing, serving ourselves up as justifications for others to do wrong, as well. Turning ourselves into robbers, we have become the victims of our own actions, for we have made ourselves less than human.

As we study the Ten Commandments, let us recommit ourselves to what ought to be among the simplest of its charges. If we be not burglars, let us also not steal copyrighted music or software. If we be not armed robbers, let us also not steal from our employers or from our nation. And let every single one of us who employs another person, even in our own homes, commit ourselves to filing the proper forms and paying the required payroll taxes. Yes, it's a pain in the neck. No, we're not likely to get caught if we don't do it. But failure to do so is a crime with victims: our employees, our neighbors, ourselves, our children, and our God.

"Thou shalt not steal" does not sound like a controversial commandment. Nor is it, really. We know that stealing is wrong. It's what we tell our children, irrespective of what we do. Thievery is against the laws of Torah, and contrary to the will of God. Let us all recommit ourselves, not just to lip service, but to adherence to the Ten Commandments and many more. Let us not steal, in any form, and let us be right with God.

Amen.

(adapted from a sermon delivered on February 17, 2006, by Rabbi Barry H. Block)

SAVOR

I batted the well-worn tennis ball against the backboard. The monotonous strokes allowed my eyes to wander to the adjoining court, where two competitors sported flashy sweats and neon yellow tennis balls fresh out of the container.

After a while, one player launched a ball clear over the fence and into the woods. The players' focus remained on their heated game, seemingly ignoring the off-course ball.

Coincidentally, my next volley sent my tattered ball to the woods as well. I exited the court and swatted my racquet back and forth against the weeds. There, amid the tall grass, lay the brand-spanking-new tennis ball.

I picked it up and admired it closely. The right thing to do would be to return the ball. But my ten-year-old brain wasn't interested in doing the right thing at that moment. Kneeling down, looking this way, then that, I very inconspicuously (so I thought) rolled the bottom of my shirt up over the ball. Next,

I positioned my hands to look like they were resting on my stomach. Suddenly, I heard a voice: "I believe that ball belongs to us." My palms began to sweat. My heart pounded. My face flushed. I was busted! Too ashamed to make eye contact, I gradually unraveled my shirt, revealing my contraband. I tossed the ball over the fence to its proper owner. Then I quickly gathered my stuff and rode my bike home in tears.

Sweaty palms, upset stomach, and heart palpitations were signals from my body that something was not going well in the Master Control Center of my brain. God placed within me the knowledge of right and wrong. He also gave me the freedom to choose. I knew the right thing to do. But I had chosen to do wrong. In doing so, I broke one of God's commandments: "Thou shalt not steal."

Fortunately, those feelings within me that summer day were strong enough to make a lasting impression. I never attempted theft again.

Sometimes, though, the urge may be too great, the desire too strong, the feelings too intense. We begin to rationalize our wrongdoing: "They are rich. They have several other balls. My ball is old and tattered. So, really, I deserve this ball." But stealing is stealing.

God isn't a dictator or control freak burdening us with loads of rules and regulations. Rather, he is a loving Father, setting up boundaries for our own well-being.

("Rules of Play" by Mary DeMent, used by permission)

Discuss Mary DeMent's article. Ask:
- *Does this story bring any personal experience to mind?*
- *How do we defend or justify such behavior?*
- *Would we act differently if we could visualize Jesus right there with us? If so, how?*

EXPERIENCE

According to a recent Barna Research poll, 4 out of every 5 teenagers (80%) had engaged in some type of music piracy in the previous six months. Furthermore, active church attenders (78%) were just as likely as non-attenders (81%) to engage in piracy. Those describing themselves as born-again Christians (77%) were just as likely to do it as non-born-again Christians (81%).

Look into it
- Donald Miller, *Blue Like Jazz*
- Rick Rusaw and Eric Swanson, *Living a Life on Loan*
- bible.com/bibleanswers_result.php?id=227
- www.worldnetdaily.com/news/article asp?ArtIcLe_ID=52332

Play the Episode 36 (Lesson 10) clip from the Faith Café DVD. Ask:
- *What thoughts were evoked in you by the Down-here song "Little Is Much"?*
- *How does this song encourage you to see the roles of both you and God in your spiritual growth?*
- *What do the words of this song say to the person who does feel overwhelmed by the commands of God?*

WALK

"You cannot serve both God and Money."
—Matthew 6:24

"A man's life does not consist in the abundance of his possessions."
—Luke 12:15

Have a brainstorming session. Make two columns on the board. Label both at the top with the words Most Wanted. In the first column, have the group write up things that most of us want (e.g. bigger homes, new cars, clothes, money, or vacations). For the second column, brainstorm about what groups in your church or local community have needs. This could be a particular ministry, such as the children's ministry, or perhaps a local charity organization. Select one group to focus on, then write ideas in the column of things that group would most want. Discuss practical ways your group might be able to provide some of these most wanted items.

Stop living to satisfy your own wants, and decide to make life and ministry less complicated for others. Think of ways your Faith Café group could make things easier for another group in your church.

- Help stock the food pantry by adding a couple items to your grocery list.
- Spend a trip to the mall looking for items to make the church nursery and children's classrooms more inviting.
- Give your time. Volunteer to help take sick church members to hospital visits, or to visit homebound patients.

This week's spiritual discipline is making room:
Think about this week's discipline as turning our obstacles into opportunities. The discipline of making room is about giving other people, fresh ideas, new experiences, and, most importantly, God the chance to do things that make our lives richer, fuller, and stronger. Instead of criticizing a church service, what about opening yourself up to see what God has for you that day? Instead of spending time stealing, lusting, or complaining, what if you paused to praise God and to invite him to take up more room in your life?

"He who holds the ladder is as bad as the thief."
—*German Proverb*

"A thief believes everybody steals."
—*Edgar Watson Howe,*
American editor and writer

Lies: Truth and Consequences

SUPPLIES NEEDED

Paper and pens or pencils

White board or chalkboard

Dry-erase markers or chalk

Faith Café DVD

ENTER

Here is your question for this week: What are "white lies"?

When is the last time you used a little deception to your advantage? Never? Come on, are you telling the truth right now?

White lies are just that—lies. They are also this—wrong. God is a God of truth. Jesus identified himself as truth incarnate (John 14:6). A lie is an affront to the very nature of the Father and the Son.

But what if we need to tell a little fib to avoid major conflict? What if our boss demands that we add a little deception for the company's good?

Rather than letting our feelings control what we learn this week, let's read what God's Word says. Remember, this is God's command.

Try this activity to get your group talking about today's subject. Construct a human polygraph machine. Pass out paper and pens or pencils. Have each group member number her paper from 1 to 10 and then write True or False in response to the statements you read out (below). Once everyone is finished, collect the papers to read out as many as time allows (with the permission of the responders, of course).

Before reading them, draw a horizontal line across the board. Write Truthful *above the line and* Deceptive *below the line. As you read through each one of a person's responses, have the group members raise their hands according to how many believe that response is truthful or deceptive. Draw a continuous line (like on a graph) to show how the responses vary from being thought of as truthful or deceptive. (For instance, if eight out of ten of your group members think Bob answered number 1 truthfully, you would draw Bob's line going up very high on the truthful side. But then if five out of ten thought he answered number 2 deceptively, Bob's line would plummet down a little over midway into the deceptive side.) Draw a new line for each responder. Or if you have enough different-colored markers or chalk, use a different color for each person so you can compare all the lines at the end for fun. You could even give a funny prize to the persons who are found to be the greatest truth-tellers or biggest deceivers (such as "white lie chocolate-covered pretzels" or "dried true-blue berries").*

Here are the statements:

1. I have taken a shower every day this week.

2. I always obeyed everything my mother told me to do.

3. I never received a spanking.

4. I am the smartest person in our group.

5. I love to hear myself sing.

6. I rarely speed on the highway.

7. I have never disobeyed any of the Ten Commandments.

8. I am amazed at how good-looking I am.

9. I really do believe God made me in his image.

10. What I've learned about the Ten Commandments has helped me understand what God wants for me.

We often want to escape the consequences of our actions and thoughts by denying them. Imagine that each of these groups of people below had just one question to ask you that you had to answer completely and honestly. In each case, what would you not want to be asked?

- Your spouse or best friend
- Your parents
- Your boss
- An IRS auditor
- A police officer
- Your children or other young relatives
- Your friends at Faith Café

Consider it

"No man has a good enough memory to be a successful liar."

—Abraham Lincoln

See if anyone is willing to share a story from their lives about a time when they were caught in a lie because their memory betrayed them. Ask: Do we normally lie because we think it will be the easy way out? Does it ever actually work out that way?

DRINK

You shall not give false testimony against your neighbor.
—Exodus 20:16

No lies about your neighbor.
—Exodus 20:16 *(The Message)*

Do not go about spreading slander among your people. Do not do anything that endangers your neighbor's life. I am the LORD.
—Leviticus 19:16

Remember that the Ten Commandments are a summary of God's laws for a nation. The ninth commandment is the basis of the justice system of that nation. Perjury is outlawed because it keeps the courts from meting out justice. But the commands to be truthful impact every aspect of a godly society, in and out of the courtroom.

GO DEEPER

In this week's episode we're studying the ninth commandment from Exodus 20:16 (also see Deuteronomy 5:20). "Bearing false witness" or "giving false testimony" prohibits lying under oath in a court of law (perjury). Sadly, this happens all the time—watch *Divorce Court* or *Judge Judy* on TV. It's often obvious that someone is lying because the person's own testimonies contradict each other! In the Old Testament civil law, there is a stiff penalty for perjury (Deuteronomy 19:16-21), which results in the perjurer receiving the punishment that was originally planned for the supposed offender.

However, this commandment has broader implications. What some people call "character assassination" likely comes under this law's condemnation as well. Injuring a person's reputation through malicious gossip, even though not in a legal setting, is a form of false testimony. Leviticus 19:16 (shown above) forbids the spreading of slander.

A literal observance and enforcement of the ninth commandment would go a long way toward cleaning up a lot of office and church gossip! Of course, the New Testament has something to say about this as well. Check out 2 Corinthians 12:20, for example: "I am afraid that when I come I may not find you as I want you to be, and you may not find me as you want me to be. I fear that there may be quarreling, jealousy, outbursts of anger, factions, slander, gossip, arrogance and disorder."

(Adapted from text by Dr. Tony Moon, professor, Emmanuel College School of Christian Ministries.)

SAVOR

After graduating from high school and starting college, Kyle loved his new life. He knew how to make friends and fit in. Professors enjoyed having a respectful student with a good sense of humor in class. Girls—many girls—thought Kyle was their kind of guy. And almost everyone else felt accepted by Kyle. His interests in music, literature, movies, and church allowed him to fit in a variety of places.

One night, after eating dinner with a few friends at a restaurant, a random comment brought back the bad memory of a big mistake. Kyle had not thought about the situation in five years.

At the restaurant, two students walked by and nodded goodbye to Kyle. Seeing them got his attention. Those two friends always walked with a third student. But now he saw only two and wondered what had happened to the other.

Kyle asked a friend if he knew why the third friend was absent. The response came as a surprise to Kyle: "They caught him cheating on a bunch of exams. Not in just one class, either. I mean, they have proof of what he did. He's gone. He lied at first and even tried to pass off the blame onto his best friends, but when the dean discovered more evidence, he was dismissed. He's gone for good. What a jerk."

Kyle said nothing, an unusual response for him. He felt shocked when emotions of disappointment and regret flooded him. He stayed around for a while, then Kyle went to his room. Alone. Quiet. Thinking. His stomach was upset.

If his high school friends had really known . . . if his parents had known . . . if his college buddies knew . . . what would they think about him now?

For the first time in a long time, Kyle felt like a liar. With his lamp on and his Bible open, Kyle tried to read. He couldn't settle his mind enough to concentrate. He decided to talk to his favorite professor the next day and tell him everything. Kyle was afraid, but he could not hold on to the deceit any longer.

As his roommate came in, Kyle pretended to be asleep.

Discuss Kyle's story:
- *Discuss times when you have been faced with painful memories.*
- *What do you think was Kyle's big mistake?*
- *What kinds of secrets would make Kyle's deception a big deal in our culture? What kinds of things would be seen as not such a big deal?*
- *How do we avoid dwelling on past mistakes? What should we do to deal with things we did wrong in the past?*

EXPERIENCE

In her 2003 annual report to Congress, National Taxpayer Advocate Nina E. Olson gave a rough estimate of the amount of tax money that was not paid due to people cheating on their taxes. According to her office, the annual gap between what taxpayers owed and what they actually paid totaled $311 billion in 2001. What do you think? Does the deception of others affect you in any way?

Play the Episode 37 (Lesson 11) clip from the Faith Café DVD. At the conclusion of the clip, engage the audience in a discussion based on speaker and author Nate Larkin's interview. Ask some of these questions:
- *"Isolation breeds deception." What do you think this quote means? Do you agree? Why or why not?*
- *Why do you think the Samson Society (the group Nate Larkin organized) has been successful? (For more information on the Samson Society see the Web address listed below.)*
- *Does Nate Larkin inspire you to be a person of honesty and character? If so, why?*

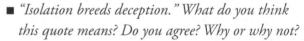

Look into it
- Os Guinness and Virginia Mooney, *When No One Sees: The Importance of Character in an Age of Image*
- Nate Larkin, *Samson and the Pirate Monks: Calling Men to Authentic Brotherhood*
- www.samsonsociety.org/Samson/home.html
- www.totalforgiveness.net/

WALK

"If a hostile witness stands to accuse someone of a wrong, then both parties involved in the quarrel must stand in the Presence of GOD before the priests and judges who are in office at that time. The judges must conduct a careful investigation; if the witness turns out to be a false witness and has lied against his fellow Israelite, give him the same medicine he intended for the other party. Clean the polluting evil from your company. People will hear of what you've done and be impressed; that will put a stop to this kind of evil among you."

—Deuteronomy 19:16-20 *(The Message)*

God held the people of Israel to a high standard of honesty. What if you were held to that standard? What would your dishonesty cost you?

This week, speak positive and honest things about another person.

- Talk directly to the person about herself.
- Be authentic. Speak the truth to this person about all the good you see in him: things he's said, things he's done, who he is.

This week's spiritual discipline is sacrifice: Sacrifice is a spiritual discipline of choosing not to demand our own way. Surrendering preferences allows us to dive deeper into the Christlike life. This week practice the discipline of sacrifice. Choose to say no to self. Just choose to do that. Not to earn God's favor, but to experience God's method of dying to live and sacrificing to gain.

NOTES

Greed: Gotta Have It

SUPPLIES NEEDED

Magazines, poster board, tape, and scissors

Store catalogs

Faith Café DVD

Paper and pens or pencils

ENTER

Thou shalt not covet.

If only I had this. If only I could do that. If only this had not happened to me. If only that person had treated me better. If only I could get married. If only I hadn't gotten married. If only I could find a better job. If only I could keep a job. If only I had a nicer car. If only I had a car. If only . . . If only I had more.

These thoughts or similar ones may be swirling in our minds as we enter Faith Café. We are here because we want to know and trust God more in our lives. Yet what do these thoughts say about what we *really* think? Do we believe God has not given us what we need? Is he unaware or indifferent to our needs? Or does the problem lie elsewhere?

Before your meeting, gather a variety of magazines. Make sure you have some that are directed to male and female audiences. In your group, pass out the magazines. Let the group members page through them and ask these questions:

- *What do you see in these magazines that represents something you want? Maybe it's something you don't have, or something you have, but want more of.*

- *Are there things that you see in these magazines that make you think, "If I had that, I'd be happy," or "If I had that, I'd feel some relief." What are those things? Why do you feel that way?*

Let each group member cut out one or two pictures that represent something he or she wants and have them tape those to the poster board. Once everyone has taped their pictures to the board, write at the top, We shall not covet?

Discontent can shape our actions and attitudes. Consider areas in which you believe that your life is unsatisfying or unfair. Ask yourself:

- In what areas of life do I feel someone else is holding me back? Is my boss out to get me? Is my family unsupportive? Or is there something I should be doing differently?

- In what areas of my life do I feel trapped by past events I cannot change?

- In what ways do I feel that lack of material resources stands in the way of my happiness?

Consider it

"Rulers do not reduce taxes to be kind. Expediency and greed create high taxation, and normally it takes an impending catastrophe to bring it down."

—Charles Adams, economist

Discuss the Consider it *quotation.*

- *What does your group think about this quote? How can greed create high taxation?*
- *It's easy to complain about the state of our economy right now, or the quality of cheap goods, or the falling house market, but do you think we as consumers bear any responsibility for these situations?*
- *How can we be more responsible in our buying habits?*

DRINK

You shall not covet your neighbor's house. You shall not covet your neighbor's wife, or his manservant or maidservant, his ox or donkey, or anything that belongs to your neighbor.

—Exodus 20:17

What shall we say, then? Is the law sin? Certainly not! Indeed I would not have known what sin was except through the law. For I would not have known what coveting really was if the law had not said, "Do not covet."

—Romans 7:7

Notice that this final commandment differs from the other nine. They all focus on behavior. This one focuses upon the attitude that is at the root of behavior. Consider how control of greed would eliminate the actions described in the other commands.

GO DEEPER

The tenth commandment (Exodus 20:17; Deuteronomy 5:21) is a prohibition of greed. It may be seen to focus especially on greed that is intense enough to produce unethical (and maybe even illegal) actions to obtain property that does not belong to oneself. "Coveting" another man's wife here is probably a reference to adulterous desires and therefore, in part, repeats the seventh commandment.

Isn't it interesting how this commandment focuses on desires rather than actions? Is this Old Testament "thought crime" legislation? The New Testament contains a much stronger emphasis on the inner aspects of sin and holiness. After all, it is sinful desire that produces sinful behavior.

The Lord Jesus himself stressed the internal origin of sin and holiness. See, for example, the verses below.

"Blessed are the pure in heart, for they will see God."

—Matthew 5:8

"You brood of vipers, how can you who are evil say anything good? For out of the overflow of the heart the mouth speaks. The good man brings good things out of the good stored up in him, and the evil man brings evil things out of the evil stored up in him."

—Matthew 12:34, 35

"Woe to you, teachers of the law and Pharisees, you hypocrites! You clean the outside of the cup and dish, but inside they are full of greed and self-indulgence. Blind Pharisee! First clean the inside of the cup and dish, and then the outside also will be clean."

—Matthew 23:25, 26

"From within, out of men's hearts, come evil thoughts, sexual immorality, theft, murder, adultery, greed, malice, deceit, lewdness, envy, slander, arrogance and folly. All these evils come from inside and make a man 'unclean.'"

—Mark 7:21-23

Before sin shows its ugly head in the form of behavior, it already exists in the human heart in the form of sinful desires, attitudes, motives, thoughts, and feelings. Hence the wisdom of Proverbs 4:23: "Above all else, guard your heart, for it is the wellspring of life."

The tenth commandment has a special relevance today when capitalist greed and the "prosperity gospel" message are consuming some sectors of the Christian movement in America and elsewhere. Jesus warned us, "Watch out! Be on your guard against all kinds of greed; a man's life does not consist in the abundance of his possessions" (Luke 12:15).

(Material from Dr. Tony Moon, professor, Emmanuel College School of Christian Ministries)

———————●———————

Bring a variety of store catalogs to your meeting. Let the group take some time to look through them. Discuss how the marketing scheme for each company promotes greed. Ask:

- *What makes these possessions seem so appealing in general? Why are they appealing to me in particular?*
- *What strategies can we use to resist the lure?*
- *What things might we focus on instead of these possessions to find contentment in our lives?*

SAVOR

Dear Moses,

This is the last one. At least for now, the rules are finished. You are now holding commandment number ten, and you can walk back into the crowd to tell them what you have been told.

How? I wonder. How can you bear to leave the moment, the experience, the listening? This has been Jehovah talking to you. You have been with the God who is too holy to be seen, whose name is too holy for full pronunciation. God, the One and Only.

And he has taken you aside and spoken powerful words to you: the Ten Commandments. They teach us and warn us. They began in your world as words to your people. They now have entered our world as guidance for modern life.

This is the last one. Number ten. What an interesting command it is.

God told you to tell your people not to be envious of what others had, whether it was a beautiful wife, a field full of cattle, or a large bank account. Instead of envy, God wants contentment. Instead of a greedy lust for more, God wants satisfaction. Instead of always wishing for a better life, God argues that by choosing appreciation for what we already have, then maybe we can truly enjoy life better.

What did you think when he spoke this command? Any guilt in your heart? Did you ever miss Egypt? Have you ever thought about how your life would have been if you had stayed in the palace? If you'd just minded your own business?

Did you ever feel a little envious of what others had?

I have. I try not to. But sometimes I do.

Today, I hope to become more content. I choose to pray, asking my Commander to be the Corrector and Protector. I'm asking your God and my God to enable me to obey him.

He promised me he would. I just need to ask.

Thanks again, Moses. I know life wasn't easy for you, but the rules from God, the ones you brought down from the mountain, make life so much better.

If only . . . we obey.

EXPERIENCE

"Human jealousy is a sign of fear. Often, it indicates immaturity, or a maladaptation of the ability to love. God's jealousy is a different matter, more like mother-love, the protective zeal of a lioness or mother bear for her young."

—Kathleen Norris, *Amazing Grace:*
A Vocabulary of Faith

Look into it

- Eric Brende, *Better Off: Flipping the Switch on Technology*
- Richard Foster, *Freedom of Simplicity*
- James Mulholland, *Praying Like Jesus*
- www.bloodwatermission.com/
- www.christianitytoday.com/le/2006/003/7 33.html

Play the Episode 38 (Lesson 12) clip from the Faith Café DVD. At the conclusion of the video clip, discuss the Jars of Clay interview. Give the group time to offer their thoughts. Ask:

- *Is it important for Christian celebrities like Jars of Clay to support organizations that help others? Why or why not?*
- *Are service and giving parts of your life? Why or why not?*
- *What do you think keeps the average American Christian from helping take care of the needs of others?*
- *If Jesus lived among us today, what do you think his response would be to those who hunger and suffer?*

WALK

This week, ask yourself a few questions: What makes possessions so appealing? How can I resist the temptation of materialism? How can I avoid purchasing things I do not need when others need so much?

Try the following assignments for the coming week:

- Day One: Thank God for what he has given me.
- Day Two: Thank God for protecting me from things I don't need.
- Day Three: Ask God to help me become a more grateful person.
- Day Four: Ask God to bless those who are wealthier than I am.
- Day Five: Ask God to bless those who have less than I do.
- Day Six: Do an act of service for someone else.
- Day Seven: Rest and meditate alone with God.

This week's spiritual discipline is leaving a legacy:

Think of a famous ballplayer saying it is time to retire. If he has done his job well, he and his team have already used their organizational skills to have the next player ready when this one says goodbye.

Experienced players guide the newcomers. Young players bring a new perspective and fresh energy. Together, both sides make the team better. Such teamwork makes each individual player better.

We should live that way as Christians too. Strategically and intentionally being mentored and mentoring others. Are you leaving a legacy because of what you own, or because of who you are? What's your legacy?

NOTES

Remember: Don't Deceive Yourself

SUPPLIES NEEDED

Communion elements

White board or chalkboard

Dry-erase markers or chalk

Faith Café DVD

ENTER

Remember how freeing it was to finish that last final exam? Remember the rush of completing a complicated business decision when a lot was at stake? Remember your anticipation as you waited for the big game? Remember the childlike excitement of waiting for snow?

Our lives are filled with events, memories, and lessons. Some memories are comforting. Some memories are useful. Memories are a gift that allow past experience to influence future endeavors.

Let this week be a reminder of where we want to go with God. Let us welcome a deeper relationship with him. May we rejoice as we realize we are going where travelers can journey only by the strength of God. As we recall his lessons for us, may we hear his voice, welcome the dare, and embark on the pilgrimage.

> *"I remember your ancient laws, O LORD,*
> *and I find comfort in them. . . .*
> *In the night I remember your name, O LORD,*
> *and I will keep your law. . . .*
> *Oh, how I love your law!*
> *I meditate on it all day long. . . .*
> *Trouble and distress have come upon me,*
> *but your commands are my delight."*
> —Psalm 119:52, 55, 97, 143

How good is your memory? Can you recall:

- the name of your first grade teacher?
- the birthdates of three relatives not members of your immediate family?
- the topic of your minister's sermon last Sunday?
- the winners of the Super Bowl five years ago?
- the names of everyone in Faith Café right now?
- the words to your high school fight song? (or even if your high school had a fight song?!)

Which of these are the most important to remember? Which are relatively insignificant?

Consider it

"I believe you can remember the future as much as the past."

—Meredith Brooks, musician

Discuss with your group:
- *What do you think she means by saying this?*
- *How can bearing your past firmly in mind help to shape your future?*

DRINK

Do not merely listen to the word, and so deceive yourselves. Do what it says. Anyone who listens to the word *but does not do what it says is like a man who looks at his face in a mirror and, after looking at himself, goes away and immediately forgets what he looks like.*

—James 1:22-24

GO DEEPER

James was a half-brother of Jesus—they shared the same biological mother. As we look at the words of both these men, we can see how well they work together. Jesus, in the Sermon on the Mount and elsewhere reveals a deeper meaning of the Old Testament laws and commands. He describes an attitude of love that should be the foundation for all of our behavior toward our family, our neighbors, and our God. James offers instructions and encouragement for practical applications of those laws and that love.

Read the following chart to the participants or make a copy of this material on a screen or a board for everyone to see. People could take turns reading the commands and Jesus' words.

The Ten Commandments said . . .	Jesus said . . .
You shall have no other gods before me. —Exodus 20:3	*Worship the Lord your God, and serve him only.* —Matthew 4:10
You shall not make for yourself an idol. —Exodus 20:4	*No servant can serve two masters.* —Luke 16:13
You shall not misuse the name of the LORD your God. —Exodus 20:7	*Do not swear at all; either by heaven, for it is God's throne . . .* —Matthew 5:34
Remember the Sabbath day by keeping it holy. —Exodus 20:8	*The Sabbath was made for man, not man for the Sabbath. So the Son of Man is Lord even of the Sabbath.* —Mark 2:27, 28
Honor your father and your mother. —Exodus 20:12	*Anyone who loves his father or mother more than me is not worthy of me.* —Matthew 10:37
You shall not murder. —Exodus 20:13	*Anyone who is angry with his brother will be subject to judgment.* —Matthew 5:22
You shall not commit adultery. —Exodus 20:14	*Anyone who looks at a woman lustfully has already committed adultery with her in his heart.* —Matthew 5:28
You shall not steal. —Exodus 20:15	*If someone wants to sue you and take your tunic, let him have your cloak as well.* —Matthew 5:40
You shall not give false testimony. —Exodus 20:16	*Men will have to give account on the day of judgment for every careless word they have spoken.* —Matthew 12:36
You shall not covet. —Exodus 20:17	*Be on your guard against all kinds of greed.* —Luke 12:15

(from Life Application Bible, © 1988, 1989, 1990, 1991 by Tyndale House Publishers, Inc.)

Discuss how James's words relate to the commandments and to the teaching of Jesus.

If anyone considers himself religious and yet does not keep a tight rein on his tongue, he deceives himself and his religion is worthless. Religion that God our Father accepts as pure and faultless is this: to look after orphans and widows in their distress and to keep oneself from being polluted by the world.

—James 1:26, 27

You believe that there is one God. Good! Even the demons believe that—and shudder.

—James 2:19

With the tongue we praise our Lord and Father, and with it we curse men, who have been made in God's likeness. Out of the same mouth come praise and cursing. My brothers, this should not be.

—James 3:9, 10

But if you harbor bitter envy and selfish ambition in your hearts, do not boast about it or deny the truth. Such "wisdom" does not come down from heaven but is earthly, unspiritual, of the devil. For where you have envy and selfish ambition, there you find disorder and every evil practice.

But the wisdom that comes from heaven is first of all pure; then peace-loving, considerate, submissive, full of mercy and good fruit, impartial and sincere. Peacemakers who sow in peace raise a harvest of righteousness.

—James 3:14-18

You want something but don't get it. You kill and covet, but you cannot have what you want. You quarrel and fight. You do not have, because you do not ask God. When you ask, you do not receive, because you ask with wrong motives, that you may spend what you get on your pleasures.

—James 4:2, 3

Anyone, then, who knows the good he ought to do and doesn't do it, sins.

—James 4:17

SAVOR

When we get caught for the bad things we do, we don't usually have to pay. The mass media are rife with examples of life without consequences. When celebrities say or do something inappropriate, they aren't held accountable for these decisions. The solution for them is typically rehab, where after four to six weeks away from their "normal" lives, their misconduct has all been washed away. . . .

God designed his plan for our benefit: to lead us toward him, not away from him; and although there is a universe of grace, compassion, and forgiveness in him, there is also an utter unwillingness to accept sin. You can break the law . . . but it is going to cost you. Keep in mind that this point is not debatable; my premise is supported in Galatians 6:7, 8 (from *The Living Bible*):

Don't be misled. Remember that you can't ignore God and get away with it: a man will always reap just the kind of crop he sows! If he sows to please his own wrong desires, he will be planting seeds of evil and he will surely reap a harvest of spiritual decay and death; but if he plants the good things of the Spirit, he will reap the everlasting life which the Holy Spirit gives him.

In an effort to help our minds comprehend God's principles against the backdrop of modern culture, let's look at the following passage from Genesis 2:24. *The Message* says, "Therefore a man leaves his father and mother and embraces his wife. They become one flesh." Theologically, it seems that upon having sex during the consummation of marriage, man and woman are joined, by God's design, in a uniquely spiritual manner meant only for husbands and wives.

But what happens when men and women participate in sex outside of marriage? God's laws are not ever altered by our interpretations of right and wrong. When men and women participate in sex outside of marriage, I believe the same spiritual connection occurs, but it is a "mutant one," not based in God's original design. Imagine that every time you have sex with someone, a spiritual connection occurs, binding the two of you together. But what if you don't stop there, but you continue to have sex with people in the free manner that our culture espouses as normal? Now imagine that these spiritual connections can be seen like monofilament fishing line. In time you would be spiritually connected to dozens of other people, not to mention those to whom they have spiritual connections. It's no wonder people who live like this often end up in an emotional and sometimes physical mess.

You can break a nail, and maybe one day we'll even break the laws of physics . . . but you can't break God's laws without consequences.

("You Can't Break the Law"
by Charles Powell, used by permission.)

Play the Episode 39 (Lesson 13) clip from the Faith Café DVD, which features The Isaacs performing "It Is Well." Share the following comments and questions with your group.

Horatio Spafford wrote the words to this hymn after several years of trial and sorrow. In 1871 he and his wife were mourning the loss of their son when the Great Chicago Fire destroyed almost all of his property. Two years later he lost all four of his daughters in a shipwreck as they traveled ahead of him to England. According to the story, he wrote the verses as he later crossed the Atlantic, passing the place where his children had died.

- *What part of the song did you like best? Which words speak to you?*
- *How can listening to the words of this song help you keep proper perspective?*
- *Does knowing Christ paid for your sin motivate you at all to live a better life?*

EXPERIENCE

"Father, it is humbling to have been granted the privilege of calling you 'Friend.' We could worship you gladly and serve you willingly if we were allowed to call you only 'Lord,' but your commitment to and interest in us goes as wide and deep and high and long as your love for us, and you express it generously in a personal relationship with us. Thank you, Father."

—Tim Stark, Emmanuel College instructor

Look into it

- David Benner, *Sacred Companions*
- Doug Pagitt, *Reimagining Spiritual Formation*
- Eugene Peterson, *A Long Obedience in the Same Direction*
- www.soulcare.com/
- www.vanguardchurch.com/spiritual formation.htm

WALK

"You have heard that it was said, 'Love your neighbor and hate your enemy.' But I tell you: Love your enemies and pray for those who persecute you, that you may be sons of your Father in heaven. He causes his sun to rise on the evil and the good, and sends rain on the righteous and the unrighteous. . . . Be perfect, therefore, as your heavenly Father is perfect."

—Matthew 5:43-45, 48

This week, begin a discipleship notebook.

- Recall the lessons of the past and learn to apply them by keeping a record of what you have studied.
- You may include sermon notes, prayer lists, memory verses and more.
- Write down goals for where you want to be in your relationship with God.

This week's spiritual discipline is remembering: These lessons took us back in time to remember, to learn, and to apply truth. Christ wanted his death to remain in our minds, our hearts, and our lives. So he instituted a time of remembrance. Think about the meaning of the Lord's Supper. Think about times you have received Communion and prepare for the next time. Confess your sins and receive his forgiveness afresh. If you are not yet a Christian, recall the messages of the episodes we have been working through. Remember the most important message is that God loves you and wants to help you. Remember who you are and who Christ is—remember what he sacrificed and the power of his resurrection.

The Emerging Church Must See Generations Connecting

By Dan Kimball

"Remember your leaders, who spoke the word of God to you.
Consider the outcome of their way of life and imitate their faith."

—Hebrews 13:7

I met Stuart Allen when I was in my early twenties, living in London and playing drums for a rockabilly-punk band. Stuart was pastor of a tiny church in London, a church in which the average age of his parishioners must have been seventy. We met when I wandered into this church one afternoon during a small lunch-hour Bible study. Stuart took me under his wing. Picture this unlikely combination: an eighty-three-year-old man,

and me, dressed all in black with a very tall pompadour, spiked wrist bands, a metal belt, a skull bolo tie, and thick-soled Creeper shoes. Stuart never seemed to see any of that. He looked right past my exterior and showed me Jesus. And it didn't matter to me whether Stuart dressed in the latest fashion or whether he knew all the bands I was interested in. What mattered to me was that he loved God and that he unconditionally cared about and loved me.

Some weekends Stuart and his wife would invite me to stay at their house in the countryside. I saw how he would wake before dawn and pray in a chair in his living room. I saw how he treated his wife with respect and love. I saw how he loved the Scriptures and memorized them.

And I was embraced by the tiny group in Stuart's church. On Sundays after the service, all fifteen of us would descend into a rather

cold and dank basement for lunch and tea. I enjoyed being the young one and the center of attention; they would all bring sandwiches and cookies and argue with each other over the privilege of feeding me. Every Sunday afternoon in that little, smelly basement, I experienced community with a group of elderly English people. As Stuart mentored me that year, I enjoyed an incredible intergenerational experience, which God used to change my life. A man in his eighties passed down the faith and wisdom to someone almost sixty years younger.

After that God placed Dr. John Mitchell in my life. I had the privilege of meeting with him almost weekly while I was a student at Multnomah Biblical Seminary in Portland, Oregon. Quite honestly, I didn't think his teaching was riveting, but I found that sitting in his office listening to him pray was a life-changing experience. The advice and wisdom of Dr. Mitchell, who was over ninety when I met him, left an indelible impression. Seeing his love for the Scriptures inspired me far beyond any sermon ever could and instilled in me a love for God's Word that remains to

this day. His intimate walk with Jesus was something I can only explain as being truly supernatural.

A third major influence in my life has been Rod Clendenen, who is over eighty years old. Rod continues to show me that worship is something you do not just at a service on Sunday but all day long. He teaches, by his life, how important it is not to depend on the church for your Bible intake but to learn to feed yourself from God's Word. These lessons could never have been taught with the same impact in sermons or classes. They can be taught only through mentoring, as generations interact with one another outside of a church setting.

Each of these men, who were in their sixties, eighties, and nineties when I met them, has made a huge impact on my life. Their photographs hang on the wall in my office and frequently remind me of the lessons these men have taught and that it's possible to make it through to old age as a disciple.

Daily Bible Readings

EPISODE 27: A Man and a Nation
Day 1: Exodus 2
Day 2: Exodus 4
Day 3: Exodus 12:1-42
Day 4: Exodus 19
Day 5: Exodus 20
Day 6: 2 Corinthians 3

EPISODE 28: The Word Was God
Day 1: Matthew 3
Day 2: Luke 4:1-28
Day 3: John 20:19-31
Day 4: Philippians 2:1-18
Day 5: Philippians 3
Day 6: 2 Peter 1:3-11

EPISODE 29: Put God First
Day 1: Genesis 12:1-8
Day 2: Genesis 35:1-15
Day 3: Psalm 96
Day 4: Acts 5:1-16
Day 5: Galatians 5
Day 6: Revelation 4

EPISODE 30: What Else Am I Worshiping?
Day 1: Exodus 32
Day 2: Isaiah 42:1-17
Day 3: Isaiah 44:9-20
Day 4: Acts 17:16-34
Day 5: 1 Corinthians 10
Day 6: Colossians 1:12-20

EPISODE 31: Words: What Am I Saying?
Day 1: Proverbs 18:1-10
Day 2: Ecclesiastes 5:1-7
Day 3: Micah 4:1-5
Day 4: Matthew 7
Day 5: Luke 4:1-15
Day 6: Romans 10:1-13

EPISODE 32: Work: Driven from Rest
Day 1: Genesis 1–2:3
Day 2: Exodus 31:12-18
Day 3: Mark 2:23–3:6
Day 4: John 14:15-31
Day 5: Romans 14
Day 6: Hebrews 4:1-11

EPISODE 33: Family: Do We Honor God?
Day 1: Ruth 1
Day 2: Ruth 4
Day 3: Luke 2:41-52

Day 4: Ephesians 6
Day 5: 1 Peter 2
Day 6: 1 Peter 5

EPISODE 34: Hatred: Murder in Our Hearts
Day 1: Genesis 4:1-16
Day 2: Matthew 15:1-28
Day 3: Luke 6:17-49
Day 4: James 2
Day 5: 1 John 3:11-24
Day 6: 1 John 4:7-21

EPISODE 35: Fantasy: Just One Look
Day 1: Job 31
Day 2: Proverbs 6:20-35
Day 3: Matthew 5
Day 4: 1 Thessalonians 4:1-12
Day 5: 1 Peter 4:1-11
Day 6: 1 John 2:1-17

EPISODE 36: Theft: Who Are We Cheating?
Day 1: Hosea 4
Day 2: Luke 19:1-10
Day 3: Romans 2
Day 4: Romans 13
Day 5: 1 Corinthians 6:1-11
Day 6: Ephesians 4

EPISODE 37: Lies: Truth and Consequences
Day 1: Leviticus 6:1-7
Day 2: Psalm 12
Day 3: Proverbs 6:1-19
Day 4: Proverbs 16:10-33
Day 5: 1 Timothy 3
Day 6: Titus 1:5-16

LESSON 38: Greed: Gotta Have It
Day 1: Proverbs 4
Day 2: Proverbs 15
Day 3: Matthew 6
Day 4: Matthew 23
Day 5: Luke 12:1-34
Day 6: Ephesians 5:1-21

EPISODE 39: Remember: Don't Deceive Yourself
Day 1: Matthew 4:1-11
Day 2: Matthew 10
Day 3: Luke 16:19-31
Day 4: Romans 12
Day 5: 2 Corinthians 12:1-10
Day 6: Colossians 3